how to start a home-based

Pet Grooming Business

HOME-BASED BUSINESS SERIES

how to start a home-based

Pet Grooming Business Third Edition

Kathy and Missi Salzberg

Guilford, Connecticut

To David, beloved husband, father, teacher, mentor, and business partner, whose loving spirit continues to guide us in all things.

To buy books in quantity for corporate use
or incentives, call **(800) 962-0973**
or e-mail **premiums@GlobePequot.com.**

Editorial Director: Cynthia Hughes
Editor: Mary Norris
Project Editor: Tracee Williams
Text Design: Sheryl P. Kober
Layout: Kevin Mak

ISSN: 1556-7621
ISBN: 978-0-7627-6367-2

Printed in the United States of America
10 9 8 7 6 5 4 3 2 1

Contents

Acknowledgments

We would like to thank the following individuals for providing guidance, inspiration, and information, gratefully acknowledging the ripple effect of their presence in our lives:

David G. Salzberg Jr. and Peter Salzberg, Kathy's sons and Missi's brothers; their wives, Aline and Julie Salzberg; Kathy's grandchildren and Missi's nieces and nephews, Allison, Cara, Kaitlin, Quinn, and Dylan, for their constant love and encouragement; Kathy's partner Lee Ackerman and Missi's partner Tracy Taylor, for their love and support; and our wonderful staff at the Village Groomer, for adding to our knowledge and inspiration on a daily basis.

Our friends in the pet grooming industry who so generously offered their expertise along the way: groomers Susan Viveiros, Diane Betelak, Carrie Prest, Elaine Belrose, and Toni Coppola; Intergroom Show Organizer Christine DeFilippo, mobile grooming pioneer Dina Perry, Melissa Verplank, Christina Pawlosky, and all the other colleagues who allowed us to pick their brains during the research process.

Shirlee Kalstone, Dorothy Walin, and Sam Kohl, groundbreakers of the grooming industry who paved the way for us all.

The editorial staff of the Globe Pequot Press and freelance editor Mike Urban who helped guide this third edition through the delivery process.

Four generations of four-legged customers and their devoted owners who have blessed our lives.

Introduction

When I joined my husband, David, at the Village Groomer in 1976, I had no intention of making pet grooming a lifelong career. My plan was to learn a new skill and help him out at the business he had founded in 1970. I really didn't have a commitment to being a self-employed business owner, but life stepped in and did the planning for me.

Although David dearly loved our grooming business, he also loved working in the health care field. In order to combine both occupations, he returned to school to earn a nursing degree. He was an eclectic person with omnivorous curiosity who succeeded at several occupations over the course of his life. I left my job as a newspaper correspondent to master the art of grooming, trading in my pen and notebook for a pair of scissors and a clipper. Interestingly enough, I found I could make more money by grooming pets than I did covering local government and politics. My new job soon became much more than an interesting sideline. I found I had a passion for grooming and experienced a genuine connection to the dogs and cats that came to our shop. Like falling in love, it came as a surprise. More than four decades later, that little shop David opened on Main Street has expanded three times, blossoming into a much larger facility.

As the business grew, my husband was drawn back into it, taking pride in its growth and relishing the friendships he forged with our clients and fellow pet grooming professionals. When David became seriously ill in 1994, our daughter, Missi, came into the business to help out for a while. Lo and behold, the same thing happened to her. Her heart was captured and her mind intrigued by this profession. She left the world of corporate sales and never looked back, taking over the day-to-day management of the Village Groomer as if she had been born for the job. (Come to think of it, I guess she was.) She modernized our salon and ushered our business into the 21st century.

Just like us, many of our fellow colleagues in pet grooming just happened into this line of work as well. You may have picked up this book because you are bored or unhappy in your present job and looking for an alternative way to make a living. You may be waiting for the answer to present itself, for something new to catch your fancy.

Although some folks still don't consider pet grooming a "real" job, doing it successfully can be challenging. The best groomers are always developing their skills and talents. They are on intimate terms with the beloved pets they care for, absorbing a great knowledge of animal behavior along the way. The friendships they form with pet owners are frosting on the cake; this profession is all about sharing the joy that dogs and cats bring to our lives. You don't need an Ivy League degree, you don't have to look like a supermodel, and you don't need the talent of a Michelangelo to succeed here. With love and dedication, you can build a career and a life.

If you wish to pursue a career in this field, it will be up to you to discover your own path to success. We sincerely hope this book will serve as a guide for you, explaining the current market for your services, outlining the talents and skills required for this career, and describing the methods of training. We have tried to instruct you on various aspects of setting up your business, including the legal and financial information you need to make it a reality.

You will need plenty of drive and determination to succeed in pet grooming. You will also need a special love and appreciation for our companions in this trip through life, our pets. Even though it really is fun to work with animals, a career in pet grooming is a serious business. You may be your own boss working from your home, but you will need discipline to succeed. Study the checklists throughout the book carefully and follow the steps to make sure you have sufficient resources before you launch your home-based business. Also, be sure to seek the best legal and financial advice you can afford.

Reading this book is a first step toward starting your home-based pet-grooming business. We congratulate you and sincerely hope you will find success beyond your wildest dreams, discovering an unusual and rewarding way of life in the process.

—Kathy and Missi Salzberg

Why Pet Grooming?

Are you an animal person? Does a backyard romp with your golden retriever refresh your soul? Is the sound of a cat purring your favorite lullaby? Do you find yourself telling your troubles to your poodle? Do you snuggle up to your pet in bed each night? There's no need to feel embarrassed. You have plenty of company.

We have become a nation of pet-crazy people. US consumers are spending more on their pets today than ever before. According to the 2009/2010 National Pet Owners Survey compiled by the American Pet Products Association (APPA), 62 percent of US households own a pet, which equates to 71.4 million homes. In 1988, the first year the survey was conducted, 56 percent of US households owned a pet. In 1994, we spent $17 billion on our furry, finned, and feathered friends. In 2010, that number grew to approximately $47.7 billion. Most of us only wish we could track the same kind of growth in our investment portfolios!

We tend to put our money where our hearts are. According to a recent national survey of pet owners conducted by the American Animal Hospital Association (AAHA), more than half of the 1,019 pet owners responding indicated that they would want a family pet instead of another person with them if they found themselves stranded on a deserted island. Eighty percent selected companionship as the major reason for having a pet, 72 percent said that affection is their pet's most endearing trait.

When it comes to pampering their furry babies, pet owners don't hold back. Seventy-nine percent give their pets holiday or birthday presents, 21 percent reveal that they sometimes dress their dogs, while 33 percent talk to their pets on the phone or through the answering machine. Sixty-two percent often sign letters or cards from themselves and their pets. Fifty-five percent consider themselves to be their pets' mom or dad. Why not? By now, we all know that pets are part of the family.

Pets are good for our health, helping us to relax and offering their love uncon-ditionally. Forty percent of owners say having a dog motivates them to exercise on a regular basis. Pet owners make fewer visits to the doctor than their pet-less coun-terparts. The simple act of petting an animal lowers blood pressure and stress levels, and pets increase the survival rate of people with heart problems. When it comes to our emotional health, pets make great therapists, too. In fact, dogs are becoming increasingly popular in therapy work, used in hospitals and nursing homes to lift the spirits and awaken the communication skills of the elderly and ill.

Such survey results always make interesting reading, but they don't surprise us in the least. After our family's four decades in the pet-grooming field, we know firsthand how precious pets can be to their people. We're aware that pet owners dropping off their furry babies for a day of beauty at the groomer's can be every bit as anxiety-ridden as parents leaving their human offspring at the day care center. We have even heard it remarked that a child is a good dog substitute! We know that statement sounds outrageous and may even ruffle some feathers, but that's the thing about pet ownership: It makes us lighthearted. It gives us permission to be silly. It charges up our capacity for play.

Since we embarked on our journey in this business, the pet grooming indus-try has truly come of age. When David left the teaching profession to become a groomer, we heard a lot of jokes about "going to the dogs" or "playing with the pooches" as opposed to having a *real* job. Until his death in 1996, we enjoyed run-ning a successful small business, gaining the friendship of countless four-legged friends and their human owners. We were rather unlikely entrepreneurs, "flower children" of the sixties who became respected burghers in the small-town business community and savoring many unexpected rewards in the process. With daughter Missi now at the helm, we have come full circle.

Since we opened that first little mom-and-pop shop four decades ago, the grooming industry has evolved. We now use state-of-the art equipment, most of which was nonexistent when we first began. Electric tables, force dryers that sweep moisture from the coat, labor- and water-saving bathing systems, improved clip-pers, superb scissors, computers, automatic vacuum systems for clippers, attrac-tive hair-proof uniforms, plus a plethora of products to make pets look and feel their best—all these have transformed what was once considered a hobby into an increasingly respected profession.

This ever-growing passion for pet ownership has not gone unnoticed by corporate America. Although the pet-grooming industry is still dominated by small businesses, many groomers face increased competition from the pet superstore chains, which now offer obedience classes and grooming services in addition to food and supplies. Popping up all over the country to compete with pet sitters and kennel operators are aggressively marketed corporate boarding facilities that are as streamlined and luxurious as posh hotels for humans. Despite this trend, independent pet-grooming providers continue to thrive. There's room for us all in this animal-worshipping lovefest.

Compare it to making your travel plans: You could book reservations at a Holiday Inn or choose to bunk at a quaint bed-and-breakfast. It's a simple matter of preference. Pet ownership occupies a special place in the innermost sanctuary of our hearts. Pet owners treasure a supremely personal connection when it comes to the people to whom they entrust their precious animals. Pets are part of the family and the importance of that familiar caring bond in delivering quality pet grooming can never be overstated.

Pet Services in Demand Today

The pet parade marches on; the number of pet-owning households growing every year. Economists foresee this trend continuing no matter how the economy dips or surges. Pet ownership appears to be recession-proof. Even when we refrain from travel, gourmet dining, or buying a new car, our joy in owning pets hits us where we live. Their reassuring presence adds to our enjoyment of the comforts of home. As the number of pets increases, so does the need for pet-grooming services.

With America's dog and cat population at 150 million, the grooming industry is undoubtedly on the move. At last count, there were approximately 60,000 to 80,000 pet groomers in the United States, averaging almost 5,000 pets per grooming establishment. Those are interesting statistics, but in reality, only half of this country's dogs and cats regularly visit a groomer. As the public becomes increasingly aware of the benefits of grooming to dog and owner alike, business will continue to mushroom. The truth about cats and dogs is this: They need groomers.

All dogs and cats benefit from professional grooming. Yesteryear's amusing stereotype of the froufrou "poodle parlor" has faded as owners realize that a clean, well-groomed pet is much more enjoyable to live with and love than the smelly, matted "backyard dogs" we might have known when we were growing up. Even shorthaired dogs shed and need periodic brushing, bathing, nail trimming, and ear cleaning. Longhaired and double-coated breeds need frequent brushing to reduce shedding and keep their coats from turning into tangled tumbleweeds. Longhaired cats require frequent grooming to keep them looking gorgeous, and their short-haired counterparts benefit from an occasional bath and brushout as well.

Like human haberdashery, canine coats come in all types and sizes. Their different grooming needs determine the amount of money owners will have to spend to care for them properly. Every breed of dog should visit a professional groomer at least four times a year. Most dogs shed heavily in the spring and fall, but many drop coat year-round. This is largely due to the fact that today's dogs live indoors, sharing our heated homes under artificial lighting, their coats no longer taking seasonal cues from Mother Nature.

The professional groomer learns to execute the proper trim on all breeds and to groom mixed breeds to look like the type of dog they most resemble. A monthly trip to the groomer is highly recommended for those breeds requiring the most upkeep: the Lhasa apso, shih tzu, standard poodle, Havanese, Maltese, Afghan hound,

Grooming Schedules

Requiring grooming every six weeks or so are the mini and toy poodle, miniature schnauzer, Pekingese, West Highland white and Yorkshire terriers, springer spaniel, and Portuguese water dog. An eight-week grooming schedule is advisable for the golden retriever, Irish and English setters, and such terriers as the wirehaired fox, Scottish, cairn, and Airedale. Dogs that require no haircut but need to see the groomer every eight to twelve weeks for coat upkeep include the German shepherd, collie, Samoyed, husky, malamute, keeshond, Akita, Shetland sheepdog, Newfoundland, Saint Bernard, and Bernese Mountain Dog. Smooth-coated dogs like the basset hound, bulldog, pug, beagle, Labrador retriever, Dalmatian, and Rottweiler are kept clean and odor-free by visits to the groomer at least four times a year. The amount of grooming an individual dog will need also depends on the amount of upkeep the owner is willing to provide at home between grooming appointments.

soft-coated wheaten terrier, bichon frise, Old English sheepdog, bearded collie, and American cocker spaniel. Today's trendy "designer dogs," mainly poodle mixes like the popular Labradoodle or Goldendoodle, require lots of brushing and styling too.

The remarkable array of dog breeds in all its infinite variety and the vast amount of knowledge to be learned about their care are part of the lure that draws people to a career in grooming, a unique and challenging career where the opportunity for success awaits those who have the right attitude, are willing to hone their skills and, of course, have a lifelong passion for pets.

Is This the Field for You?

You may have picked up this book because you are toying with the idea of making a career switch into the pet grooming field yourself. You may be fed up with your job in the corporate world, arising each morning to dress for success as your enthusiasm for running in place on the fast-track treadmill continues to wane. You may have been laid off and are wondering which road to take for your next life chapter. You may be a stay-at-home parent toying with the notion of combining your workplace with the comfort and convenience of being at home, or a harried commuter who spends far too many hours of your precious time on the freeway. We know bankers, lawyers, nurses, secretaries, teachers, real estate brokers, military retirees, and downsized dot-commers who now make their living caring for pets. In a 2008 Petgroomer.com survey of people seeking a career in this field, 71 percent of those who responded had never worked with pets before.

Then there is the lure of being your own boss. Recent surveys reveal that one in three Americans would prefer to earn their pay right where they live. The number of people who worked at home increased by nearly 2 million, from about 9.5 million in 1999 to about 11.3 million in 2005, according to the US Census Bureau. Nearly half of these home workers had college degrees and half earned $75,000 a year or more.

With today's mindboggling advances in technology, more and more home-based workers are added each year. These workers made up 8 percent of the total US workforce in 2005, up from 7 percent in 1999. Among those who worked at home in 2005, about 8.1 million did so exclusively, an increase from 6.7 million in 1999.

There are an estimated 29.6 million small businesses in the United States, employing just over half of the country's private sector workforce, according to SCORE, Counselors to America's Small Businesses. Home-based businesses represent 53 percent of all small firms and their piece of the pie provides 10 percent of the economy's total receipts. All in all, the nation's small businesses generate more than 52 percent of all US sales and contribute about 21 percent of all manufactured US exports. They remain the principal source of new jobs.

Sure, you'll work longer hours and probably take a hefty pay cut for the privilege of building your own business, but there is no denying the heady feeling of pride and self-esteem that comes from declaring your financial independence.

You have the desire to become an independent businessperson and the dream of working from your own home. But how do you know if pet grooming is the right choice for you?

The First Ingredient Is Love

Unlike the Beatles hit song of long ago, love is not all you need. But to succeed in this field, it is undoubtedly the first ingredient. Pet-grooming professionals must project that love. If you are cranky to an animal in front of its owner, you have just lost a customer. Pets themselves know who their friends are. They tune in to your emotions of love and kindness with an almost mystical ability. When it comes to your feelings for the animals in your care, you can't fake it.

On a day when every dog you groom is either trying to leap off your table, take a bite out of the brush and/or your hand, or bark so long and loud that your head is throbbing, you will need a truckload of patience and a mountain of maturity. When that sparkling white bichon frise you just scissored to perfection has an "accident" in its crate and must go back in the tub for another bath while its owner taps her foot waiting for you to finish, you'd better have a strong stomach and nerves of steel.

When the little pup on your table is spinning like a top as you try to brush it and trim its nails, or the canine senior citizen needs to be groomed lying down instead of standing up because her hindquarters are weakening, you will need unlimited patience and understanding. But if you are a dyed-in-the-wool animal person, such situations will probably not dissuade you. You know who you are.

Still not sure you've got the animal person gene? The following scenarios might help. Which of these ring true?

- When visitors to your home object to a little pet hair, you suggest they meet you elsewhere—or bring their own lint brush.
- When your puppy needed leg surgery, you gave up that beach house vacation rental in a heartbeat to pay the vet bill.

- When your neighbor's dog was hit by a car, no one but you could function to drive it to the vet.
- The stray cat population has designated your house a favorite stop on its mysterious underground trade route.
- Your backyard has recently become the unofficial headquarters for the neighborhood puppy play group.

Any one of these examples might be the sign you've been searching for. Your future may lie in working with animals.

This is not to infer that true "animal people" are confined to the pet grooming industry, but the best pet grooming providers we know happen to fall into this category. They share a reverence and respect for all living creatures. They seem to possess an uncanny ability to communicate with pets via a look, a touch, or a word. Being open to this human-animal energy flow is a gift, but we believe it can also be learned. Our Native American predecessors had this ability and used it well. You may suspect that we are becoming a bit too earthy-crunchy here, but working with animals is unlike working with computers, flow charts, or other inanimate objects. Attempting to explain it is like trying to use words to describe a piece of music.

As part of your research into entering this field, may we suggest some field trips? Ask if you can spend a day at a grooming salon. While observing this occupation up close and personal, you can help out by sweeping the floor or volunteering to be the gofer at coffee time. You can take it a step further by offering your services at a local shelter. There are never enough compassionate souls to care for all the homeless animals that are still a heartbreaking reality in our affluent society. You may learn that you don't have the stomach to scoop the poop, that pet hair makes you sneeze, or that the sound of all that barking makes you want to bang your head against the wall. Chalk it up to research and move on.

If you're convinced you have the animal-loving gene you're on the right road, but you've only just begun. There are some other qualities you will need. We have seen many people who could scissor and clip a poodle so exquisitely that it looked ready to take its place in the show ring and have known others whose business savvy left us in the dust, but they lacked the temperament needed for this kind of work. Many of the most talented groomers are dyed-in-the-wool animal lovers; unfortunately, not all of them have acquired the business skills needed to turn their talents into profitable careers. For such humanely oriented individuals, it's all too easy to work for insufficient financial compensation. After all, in their minds, they are performing a labor of love. Some would do it whether they got paid or not. Others have not learned that until their prices reflect that they themselves value their services, no one else will.

Although there is nothing wrong with gaining satisfaction and experiencing joy in working with pets, there is also nothing wrong with making a profit. You can feed your soul and enjoy your four-legged patrons, but you also deserve to make a living, take care of your family, and plan for a comfortable retirement. Mastering the management of your home grooming business is every bit as vital to success in this career as perfecting the art of styling the various breeds.

Many pet grooming providers fail as business owners because they do not have enough capital behind them to keep the business going until it turns a profit. Starting your own business in any field is a risky endeavor. As many as 75 percent of all new businesses fail within five years due to undercapitalization. To make it in your own pet grooming business, you will need to wear two hats: that of the knowledgeable animal lover and that of the astute businessperson.

David used to say that groomers are artists who work on the most difficult canvas of all, a living creature. With love and skill, they transform a sometimes dirty, smelly, matted dog into an attractively coiffed canine. We're not saying you will need to be a Picasso or Michelangelo to succeed at this vocation, but you will need a measure of manual dexterity.

The next ingredient in this stew is the dedication to work hard and learn every day. For instance, there were more than 168 dog breeds represented at the last Westminster Kennel Club Dog Show. A professional groomer should know the breed standard for each and every one. And despite the arrival of labor-saving tools to make the job easier, it still requires a strong and energetic person to do this type of work day in and day out.

More Than Playing with the Puppies

Although pet grooming has come a long way, there are still many people who consider it a rather amusing way to make a living. They simply can't resist hurling those clever little barbs: "What? You want to be a doggie hairdresser?" "You want to primp poodles for a living?" Being taken seriously can be a challenge in pet grooming occupations. Some people take a more starry-eyed view: "I wish I could play with the puppies all day and get paid for it!"

Well, yes, working with animals is a great way to make a living and you can have fun with your four-legged customers, but pet grooming occupations can be extremely demanding.

Groomers are prone to back problems from lifting heavy dogs, and carpal tunnel syndrome from the repetitive motion of scissoring, brushing, and hand stripping. Learning to groom sitting down on a stool is a great idea. As is the case with human hairstylists, a groomer's legs can suffer from standing all day over a long period of time. Circulation problems, varicose veins, overstressed tendons and ligaments—these are common ailments in this profession. So here's another qualification to consider: You need to be in shape as much as you need to love and respect animals.

In addition, pet grooming workers tend to get caught up in their work, sometimes to the detriment of their personal lives. You will need to balance your life so that it does not sap all your attention and energy. You easily can become such a workaholic that you may miss out on some important moments with your children: prom pictures, Little League games, school Christmas pageants. You can't have those opportunities back, but you might be able to profit from the experience of those of us who have been there, done that. If you start off strong and healthy and work smart, these occupational hazards can be avoided.

People come into this career for myriad reasons, not all of them well founded. We can't recall how many times we have heard this statement: "I want to work with animals because I can't stand working with people." Well, you've got yourself a problem. Every single one of those four-legged patrons of yours is brought in by an owner, sometimes a whole carload full of them!

People skills are a necessity. You will need them to explain why these sometimes obsessive owners should trust you to groom little Fluffy. You will need them to educate your clients about caring for their pet's coat between visits so that it doesn't resemble a bramble bush each time it comes in. You will need them to tactfully inform these folks that little Benji is sorely in need of an obedience trainer, or that he needs to be neutered so he will stop trying to leave his personal marker on every square inch of the world, including those plush new pet beds in your retail section. You will need them to explain to the harried mom that her children cannot dismantle your cookie bins and play catch with the kitty toys while she agonizes over which credit card to use.

When it comes to people skills, it's a job like any other. When you are dealing with the public—or with employees as your business grows—you will run across an amazing cross section of humans with all their stellar attributes and maddening foibles. Pet grooming is a service industry, and all service industries require the ability to interact favorably with people.

You will also need the burning desire to get the proper training. Mastering the necessary skills takes patience and perseverance. A third of professional groomers still learn to groom on the job, but there are now many grooming schools throughout the country that offer professional training. Starting out with an entry-level position like groomer's assistant or bather-brusher is a great way to familiarize yourself with the world of pet grooming before you commit your time and money to professional training.

Last but not least, you will need a thick skin. To grow and learn in this profession, you must be open to constructive criticism, from your teachers, from fellow pet grooming professionals, and even from your clients. Sure, you are bound to hear some unfounded criticism along the way, but try not to take it personally. Discard those defense mechanisms and be open to learning something new, or at least looking at your work in a new light.

Honestly Assessing Your Capabilities

Let's reexamine our list of the qualities needed to succeed in pet grooming: love for animals, good business skills, sufficient capital to get started and stay in business, physical health, the drive to work hard, people skills, the desire and commitment to master the proper skills, the dedication to keep learning and improving, a thick skin, an open mind, and, of course, a sense of humor. Pet ownership is all about joy! You will also need lots of patience and understanding for pets and owners alike in this pet-related occupation.

Those considering a career in grooming will need a good eye to be able to visualize the result they are trying to create, as well as the motor skills to produce it with clippers and scissors. Developing such skills takes time and talent, but some artistic ability and creativity are prerequisites for this job.

How did you stack up? If you think you have the right stuff, read on—and advance confidently in the direction of your dreams!

Before You Begin

Before you embark upon any journey, you need to chart your course. In the pet grooming field, there seem to be as many roads to success as there are professionals. Happily for those who aspire to this work, you can begin your training while working at another job, planning your strategy as you move toward your goal. One of the blessings of this field is that if you are serious about making a living by working with animals, doors will open as you proceed.

Training Needed

There are many training options available to those who want to get started in the pet grooming profession. Here are just a few of the opportunities that you can take advantage of.

Grooming: Apprenticeship versus Formal Training

When we began our grooming business, most groomers learned through the apprenticeship method, but there are certain limitations involved in learning on the job. The first constraint is time. In today's salon environment, it is difficult for the busy groomer to instruct a trainee. Because of the safety issues involved and the responsibility of turning out quality grooming for the paying customer, close supervision is required. This tends to cut down on shop productivity. In the grooming world, time is definitely money!

Another drawback to the apprenticeship method is that you learn only your employer's methods of grooming. If your teacher is one of the great ones, you will be fortunate; if not, you may find that you wish to grow beyond his or her level of competency.

Improving Your Skills

The grooming industry offers a wealth of opportunities for improvement through in-service training, certification programs, workshops, national and international seminars, and grooming competitions. Catch the magic as you watch the world's best groomers compete at Intergroom, an international conference held annually in April in New Jersey, www.intergroom.com, or GroomExpo, a huge event held each September in Hershey, Pennsylvania, www.groomexpo.com. Both are showcases for the latest trends in grooming products and great places to shop for your salon. In addition, there are state and regional conferences that draw the big guns of the grooming world to your locale to share their expertise. Join your state or regional grooming association and attend these conferences to open your eyes to a wonderful world that few outside our industry are aware of.

The money you invest in yourself and your career will be worth every penny. It is an eye-opener to see the leading lights of the grooming industry—superstars who regularly win trophies, ribbons, and cash prizes—attending these seminars and polishing their skills. They keep growing in this arena because they are always open to learning more. Read every book and magazine article you can get your hands on. Profit from the experience of pet grooming pioneers like Shirlee Kalstone, Sam Kohl, and Melissa Verplank.

Today, two-thirds of those planning to enter the grooming industry plan to attend a grooming school. The decision to choose the right grooming school for you should not be made lightly. Check out the schools close to you and do some surfing on the Internet to investigate other institutions, beginning with their websites. You will need to check each school's accreditation and licensing. Most states require schools to furnish contact information for the state agencies in charge of licensing vocational schools. Make sure the information is current and the school is on firm financial footing. In the mid 1990s, some unfortunate grooming students in our home state were left high and dry when the institution of their choice closed its doors due to financial problems before their courses of study had been completed. Look for a reference list of graduates you can call on for feedback.

There are many questions to ask when investigating a grooming school. These schools usually operate in conjunction with a grooming salon; find out if the number of dogs provided is sufficient for plenty of hands-on training. Will you be taught to groom all the major dog breeds, mixed breeds, and cats?

How much business training is provided? Because your goal is to start your own business, courses in business management, including the use of computer programs developed specifically for the pet industry, would be highly important to the grooming entrepreneur.

What is the ratio of students to teachers? Is it small enough to provide adequate individual attention? What about the background of the instructors? Are they experienced professionals who have achieved success in the grooming field?

If a school under your consideration is not within commuting distance, check out the availability and cost of student housing. Ask about tuition costs and whether a full kit of grooming equipment is included in this fee. Find out if financial aid, including student loans and Pell Grants, is available and if job placement is provided. Because of today's increasing shortage of trained groomers, most students should have a job waiting for them upon graduation. Although recent years have brought a recession, there are approximately 2,000 groomer job openings in the United States, some offering $50,000 or more per year. In the more than forty years we have been in business, there has been a shortage of groomers in many areas of the country. For 2010 the demand is expected to increase by 12 percent, according to Petgroomer.com.

Gathering such information should not be a struggle for the prospective student. The school should freely and enthusiastically provide it.

With established groomers competing for the pool of available talent, some busy shop owners are now sending their promising homegrown prospects to grooming school, footing the bill for an agreement to work in their employ for a specific period of time. You can also learn to groom while working for a pet superstore chain. PetSmart, one of the "big box" pet superstores, now offers training as part of its job recruitment program. Applicants must first be employed full-time for a minimum of thirty days, and the store in which they work must have the need for a pet stylist. The training usually lasts six months, after which they would be under contract to work for PetSmart for two years. Participants are trained at one of their one hundred or so "academies" within store salons, receiving the megastore's own certification upon successfully completing the course. PetSmart's groomers are required to attend at least 32 hours of safety training and must be re-certified each year. The fast-growing company plans to offer grooming at every one of its 1,100 stores in the United States and Canada.

Petco, another pet industry giant, also grows its own groomers at training centers throughout the country. Trainees start at entry level, as bather-brushers for three months, and are paid minimum wage while learning to groom under the guidance of a mentor for four months. They must also groom for two months at their home salon before training is completed. Once groomers have graduated and successfully groomed 100 dogs, they are paid a 50 percent commission. Petco now offers grooming at its 1,000 stores nationwide.

If you are receiving private instruction from an established groomer, you should be aware that it's common within the grooming industry for an employee to be asked to sign an agreement prohibiting him or her from opening a business within a certain distance from the employer. Even with this restriction, the experience of working for someone else could be extremely beneficial to the budding groomer-entrepreneur. Whether such a contract would hold up in court may vary from state to state. However, we strongly recommend that you be fully aware of your contractual obligations and that you live up to them. Burning your bridges—and those who have nurtured you along the way—is always a bad idea. Friendships are important and beneficial in this industry. Furthermore, as long as you honor your obligations to your employers and mentors, your intent to be your own boss should be perfectly understandable. True friends will celebrate your success.

Contact the schools that interest you most and request a catalog. After careful review, follow up with a visit to the school to tour the facilities and to schedule a preliminary interview with the administrators. Look for clean, modern, well-lighted instruction areas and state-of-the-art equipment. Make sure students are well-supervised and animals are treated with kindness and respect. The atmosphere should come as close to that of a professional salon as possible. Your training in this career will constitute the foundation of your success, so choose your school carefully. It is an important step in your journey to become a pet grooming professional.

This profession does not require vocational licensing, which means that there are no hard and fast rules regarding a school's curriculum. The onus is on you to find the school that best meets your individual needs.

Most grooming schools offer courses at different levels for prospective groomers, bather-brushers, or grooming assistants. Most also offer full-time, part-time, evening, and weekend training. By and large, a course of study to become a full-finish groomer would involve a minimum of 600 hours, although our search through many school websites indicated that such courses vary in length from 200 to 1,000 hours. Average tuition for a full course of study ranges from $4,000 to $8,000. Many schools offer online grooming courses but in our opinion, there should be hands-on training with real live pets. While you're building the experience needed to open your own business, you may find employment as a groomer in a variety of settings: salons, kennels, retail pet chains, veterinarian offices, or doggie day care centers.

Your Support System: Family and Friends

Starting your own business is a life-changing decision. These days, few of us stay on the same career track for our entire working lives, retiring with a gold watch and a pension after thirty or more years of service. You are probably approaching this decision with a job history as well as family connections and obligations. How you handle combining your personal and professional lives can play a huge role in whether you will be successful in achieving your goals.

Establishing a new career is a gigantic leap. Sometimes you feel like you've jumped out of the plane but you're still waiting for the parachute to open. Enlisting the aid and goodwill of those nearest and dearest to you can be a crucial factor in your success. Look upon it as your first public relations challenge. You need to make your significant others part of your team.

In the planning stages of a new business, commercial loans may not be available to you. If your own savings and other sources are insufficient for your goals, financial assistance from relatives and friends may be a great blessing to you as you get started. It is imperative, however, to keep such agreements on a strictly business basis. If you borrow money, put your loan agreement in writing and spell out how and when it will be repaid once you are in a position to draw an income. Relationships with family and friends can be permanently damaged if all such arrangements are not drawn up legally to make sure everyone's position is completely understood.

Family members will want to be included in the birth process of your new creation. Recruit their support in the planning stages by holding family meetings at which everyone gets a chance to talk—and listen. Starting any business necessarily involves some sacrifice and inconvenience, especially if family members are accustomed to being your top priority, but embarking on a home-based business brings its own set of challenges to the table. Your spouse or children may be apprehensive about possible disruptions and invasions of their privacy in that most precious of all sanctuaries, their home.

Friends will also react to the changes that starting a new business will bring. Some will cheer you on, rolling up their sleeves to help and offering support. If you let them in on the planning process, you may be amazed at their enthusiasm and their creative input. Until you pick their brains, you may have no idea of their particular areas of expertise or the connections they may have to others who can assist you.

Other friends may resent your passionate new involvement. Like any type of life-changing event, this can be a true test of friendship. It's always a good idea to listen to friends' concerns with an open mind, but the negative nonbelievers can be a drain on the motivation and confidence you need right now. It takes courage to start a business, and it takes strength to leave non-nurturing relationships behind.

The best way to gain the support of those closest to you is to include them in your vision. Listen to their concerns and fears and let them know they will be needed and included in your plans. There will be days when your attention is focused on designing and constructing your home office or shop, working on marketing, or meeting with accountants, attorneys, or local officials. These hectic days may lead to nights when take-out meals are eaten from paper plates. If your family shares your spirit of adventure, such inconveniences can be treated with a lighthearted attitude. Down the road, the success of your home-based business will become a source of family pride. It will also keep you closer to your loved ones as you work from your home.

It will not, however, be all sweetness and light. If family members will be working with you, there can be rough spots. Compare it to an office romance. There are valid reasons that management frowns upon on-the-job romantic entanglements. Combining business and personal concerns can be like playing with fire. As you forge ahead with your family business, what happens when your mate must delve into its ups and downs as you both focus on it over breakfast, lunch, and dinner?

As members of a multi-generational family endeavor, we have found that viewing the business as a process rather than an entity unto itself helps make things flow more smoothly. As a business ebbs and flows, struggles and grows, everything should be negotiable; our roles should not be carved in stone.

Can you and your mate share home-front responsibilities as you face the demands of building the business? Can you be open to discussions on why one design would work better than another without turning it into a power struggle?

Control issues can rock the boat when it comes to family members interacting on the job. What worked best for our family was a division of labor and responsibilities according to our individual strong points.

Our founder David was superb at sales, a trait his daughter Missi inherited. Their outgoing personalities fueled our retail business, drawing people to our shop like a magnet. Kathy's place to shine was the grooming room, keeping standards high and transmitting motherly love to the pets in our care, always stressing kindness and compassion while working with our staff to make our four-footed customers look and feel beautiful.

As the business grew and changed over the years, Missi's strengths as a staff manager emerged, enabling her to walk that fine line between being the boss and being a friend to our groomers. She also ushered us into the age of computerization and labor-saving equipment, allowing us to work smarter—and greener.

In a successful family business, we learn to focus on each other's strong points and encourage each other's growth. When it works the way it should, all of our special gifts and strengths can be woven together into a beautiful tapestry.

If your husband is the handyman type, his talents can be invaluable in designing and building your workspace. If your wife is a computer buff, enlisting her to set up your computer system can be a great financial boon. Your son may be a budding artist. Call upon him to design your logo, your business cards, and your brochure. Even the youngest family members can stuff envelopes, distribute flyers, or stock shelves. (A cautionary note to home groomers: If your relatives or friends are carpenters, plumbers, or electricians, by all means solicit their services to save on startup costs— but make sure the work they perform is in compliance with local building codes.)

In many family businesses, husbands and wives clock in as many as seventy to eighty hours a week on the job, working to provide a better future for themselves and their children. How do they do it without getting on each other's nerves? Sometimes it helps to have a few ground rules, such as keeping business problems out of the bedroom or not tackling tough issues over dinner. David declared business matters off-limits when we took a weekend drive to our summer camp. If you are the type of person who chews over every problem like a terrier working on a bone, this might not be an easy policy, but that weekly break became part of our routine, helping us reconnect as husband and wife, rather than as business partners.

Your home-based business can create family wealth for current and future generations. It can become an expression of your family values as you work together to make it grow. The challenges of working with family can be daunting, but the rewards are great. As you set sail upon your dream, make sure to invite the ones you love onboard!

Attitude Is Everything

Your dream is taking shape! You wake up one morning and you know deep inside it's time to be the boss, to take your future into your own hands. You feel six feet tall and bulletproof, ready to take the plunge. Wouldn't it be great if you had this positive, confident feeling all the time? Unfortunately, those moments of worry and indecision will probably come back, creeping up to nibble at your optimism like gypsy moths on your maple tree. How do you get those pesky parasites to fold their tents and stop nibbling on your confidence? You can decide to have a winning attitude every single day.

Some fortunate folks are born with that upbeat quality. They have relentless determination to succeed 24/7. The rest of us have to work at it. We all know people stuck in the "ain't it awful" mode. The weather is always too hot or too cold. The traffic is horrible. They may look like the picture of health, but they will soon fill you in on their litany of health problems. These folks always view the glass as half empty; unfortunately, their pessimism is contagious.

Work on developing an optimistic attitude. Focus on the positive aspect of every situation. At first, you may need to switch your new attitude on every morning, but eventually it will become a habit. Every problem you encounter presents an opportunity to think creatively and come up with a possible solution. Every negative individual you encounter gives you a chance to practice being positive. As Eleanor Roosevelt said, "No one can make you feel inferior without your consent."

Here are some hints to help you stay positive as you proceed:

- Get some motivational tapes and listen to them whenever you can: driving the car, exercising, folding laundry, emptying the litter box. Wayne Dyer and Tony Robbins are our personal favorites, but there is a whole industry of such inspired and inspiring speakers to bring on board as your personal coaches.
- Join business groups. Find out which ones will help you to gain clients and allow you to network with fellow businessmen and businesswomen. Attend a few meetings to familiarize yourself with the group's overall mission. Your

What It Takes to Succeed Checklist

	Completed
1. Prepare a business plan (see chapter 3), including:	
Your goals	❏
Marketing plan	❏
Competition research	❏
Financial plan	❏
Office and grooming shop plans	❏
List of equipment needed	❏
Shipping and delivery schedule for equipment	❏
Cash flow projections	❏
Growth plan	❏
2. Announce your plans to open a business to family and friends.	
(Stress confidentiality at this point in time.)	
Enlist their aid in helping you set up your business.	❏
3. Purchase a daily planner book or electronic device to track personal and professional tasks.	❏
4. Strengthen your winning attitude.	
Listen to motivational tapes.	❏
Read everything you can about pet grooming.	❏
Join business groups.	❏
5. Create a better personal reputation.	
Request and edit your credit profiles.	❏
Pay bills on time and make sure you keep your word.	❏
Treat everyone you meet with respect and courtesy— they are all potential customers!	❏

mother was right: Hanging out with the wrong crowd will bring you down to their level. Cultivate some new associates who have a winning attitude.

- Read books by successful entrepreneurs. There are many Horatio Alger stories on the bookshelves. Learning how others have overcome adversity and triumphed in business and in life will help you to follow their example.

Your Word Is Your Bond: Building a Golden Reputation

Decide from day one that you will build a superb reputation. Get in the habit of keeping your promises and meeting your financial obligations. Return phone calls and show up on time for your appointments. Your reputation precedes you in business and will last long after you have sold it or passed it on to a family member. When you decide to retire, it will have a direct bearing on what your business will be worth.

Most of us have dealt with a friend or relative who borrows money, then conveniently forgets to repay it. People like this put us in an awkward position when we have to chase them and remind them of their financial obligations. In business, it's the same scenario. Your creditors will not respect you if they have to hound you to pay your bills.

The pet grooming industry has come of age, but in its formative days it saw its share of shady characters who proved to be bad credit risks. It's up to us to put this impression to rest and gain the respect we deserve. Viewed from a more concrete perspective, if you don't pay your bills, you will soon be out of business.

Your accountant will be your right hand when it comes to financial planning. This valuable team member will advise you on managing the costs of setup and operation in the planning stages. He or she will provide you with a monthly profit and loss statement so you manage according to your cash flow, gauge your progress, and plan future expenditures.

Don't be an ostrich. If you have trouble paying a bill, hiding your head in the sand only makes things worse. Facing up to your obligations like a responsible adult will preserve your reputation and lessen your stress level. Contact the company or utility to make arrangements for a payment schedule. It goes without saying that you cannot take a salary before your business pays its bills.

These suggestions will help you to make sure your reputation is one of your greatest assets:

- Request your credit profiles from TRW/Experian (800-397-3742; www .experian.com), Equifax (800-997-2493; www.equifax.com), or TransUnion (800-888-4213; www.transunion.com). It may not be possible to erase a negative credit history, but you can review it for discrepancies and find out what information is being furnished to banks and other potential creditors. Obtain this information before you apply for a loan or request credit from your distributors.

- Take a good look at how you manage your personal finances. Do you pay your bills on time? If you regularly lose track of due dates, you must learn to live by your daily planner, whether it's a book, a Blackberry, or a smart phone. From now on, it's your bible. Enter the due dates and get those checks in the mail five days before they're due.

- Treat everyone like a potential client. Refrain from denigrating your competitors. It's disrespectful and unprofessional. Besides, someday they may send business your way, come to your aid in an emergency, or work with you on a common problem. To preserve your golden reputation, practice living by the golden rule.

The Pet Population in Your Area

You need to do your homework to determine if there is a need for the pet grooming services in your locale. The first step is to find out how many pets live in your town and the surrounding towns from which you will draw your customer base. To determine the number of dogs in any community, contact the town clerk's office to request the number of licensed dogs. For a small fee you can also get a printout of the names and addresses of their owners, pertinent data when it's time to publicize your services.

The numbers and types of other pet grooming services in your area are also a good indication of potential opportunity for your business. If there are several grooming salons as well as pet supply chains that offer grooming services, you will know that the market is being served, but that does not necessarily mean that there would not be room for one more. When you market yourself as a home-based groomer, you would need to stress what makes your services unique and desirable. It may be the warm homelike atmosphere without the hustle and bustle of a large salon, or the individual attention pets would receive, especially important to owners of senior pets with special needs. Although we have sometimes wondered whether leaving a pampered pet for grooming was more traumatic for its owner than for the pet, we know that some dogs don't do well in a setting with several other dogs. There are other pets with health issues who must get in and out as soon as possible. You can create your own niche.

Where there are people, there are pets. If you live in a populated area that supports many growing businesses of all types, chances are excellent that there is a place for the service you wish to provide. If you have the love of animals, the business skills, and the burning desire to make your living doing something close to your heart, there will be room for you in the ever growing world of pet grooming.

What's in a Name?

What will you name your baby? For parents, this is one of the most delightful decisions to mull over. For some of us, it may seem easier than picking a name for a new business!

Your business name will be one of your most important assets. In christening this new venture, you will want to pick something that reflects what you do and who you are. In our opinion, the pet grooming industry suffers from an overabundance of "cutesy" names, probably having to do with the way people baby their pets. We'll admit it; we've been known to lapse into baby talk ourselves when communicating with our own beloved animals or canine and feline customers, but if I were you, I would shy away from a name that is too cute for your new venture. "Pepi's Poodle Palace" or "Connie's Cuddly Critters" may work for you, but we prefer something that conveys a more professional image.

Another point to ponder: Humorous references can be fun, but in naming a grooming business, I would avoid the words "Dirty" or "Hairy." The picture these words call to mind is not the image you wish to convey to potential clients. For any pet grooming venture, something that relates to warmth, safety, caring, and kindness is reassuring to the pet owner searching for your services. In these times when grooming salons have morphed into pet spas, a little snob appeal doesn't hurt either. People like to think that they are providing only the best services for their beloved pets.

The name you choose should be easy to remember and should make a personal statement. It should not be difficult to spell or pronounce, and it should not resemble another company's name except in the common denominator of *Grooming*

Services. Because there is such a proliferation of pet grooming businesses today, it's a good idea to have a few names under consideration. Mull them over before you commit yourself. Run them by family and friends to solicit their opinions.

Once you have settled on a couple of favorites, check the local registry of deeds to see if anyone else in your area is using the names. You can also check your local city or town hall, the library, and the yellow pages. Your next stop is the Secretary of State's office, where you can find out if your prospective names are already in use within your state.

There are actually three types of business name categories. The one you choose will play a part in how you register or officially file your name. *Trade names* identify a specific company, like Reebok, Pepsi Cola, or Microsoft. (Any type of business can call itself a company.) *Corporate names* identify corporations. You can tell they are incorporated by the word "Incorporated," "Corporation," or "Limited" (usually abbreviated Inc., Corp., or Ltd.) after their name. You cannot legally use these terms in your name unless you are actually incorporated. If you have decided on a name for your corporation but are still in the planning stages, you can contact the corporations division in your state and reserve the name for thirty days. This will protect the name you have chosen from infringement by others while you are preparing to incorporate. In my state, this must be done in writing, and a small fee is charged for the service.

If someone else is already using the name you would like, you would, of course, be prohibited from using it. In some cases, an exemption can be made if you are able to obtain a letter of consent from the other corporation, giving you permission to use a similar name, but to avoid confusion or legal ramifications, having a name that is uniquely your own would obviously be your best bet.

Trademarks are words, symbols, or a combination of the two that identify a business and distinguish its products and services from others. The purpose of registering your name as a trademark is to protect your exclusivity. It gives you the right to bring an action against anyone who uses the same or a similar name or product. Often the name of the first producer of a product or service becomes a generic term for that item, such as Kleenex for a facial tissue or Rollerblade for in-line skates. In the early stages, when you have no competition, it may not matter if your name becomes synonymous with your product or service, but when competitors spring up and use your name as a generic term for their product or service, you are faced with a major problem.

Product names fall into generic use with the public anyway, but the battle wages on. To keep it from generic use, the Kimberly-Clark Corporation refers to its product as "Kleenex brand facial tissues," to make sure that Kleenex is the brand or trademark. Rollerblade, Inc., officially terms its product "Rollerblade in-line skates." These big companies retain a team of lawyers just to police the publishing world and protect their trademarks.

On a far smaller playing field, when we decided to call our grooming shop "The Village Groomer" back in 1969, we did not take the time to register or trademark our name. With our industry's growth, there are now at least a dozen "Village Groomers" scattered around the country. I have met some of my fellow Village Groomers at industry conventions, and sometimes we get each other's e-mails by mistake. Although we have no grounds to complain about sharing the name with these colleagues, it would have been wiser to plan ahead and have taken the time to protect the name we gave "our baby" all those years ago.

You can determine if there is a federal trademark on a name you are considering by contacting the United States Patent and Trademark Office (PTO) in Washington, D.C. You can do trademark research yourself, or hire an attorney specializing in patents and trademarks. The search option is available to you at any federal depository library, with branches in all fifty states. Call (800) 786-9199 for the nearest location, or log on to the PTO website at www.uspto.gov/trademarks/index.jsp. In some cities, there are trademark search services available for a fee. Some public libraries will perform a computerized search for you, also usually involving a small fee.

Once you receive your forms from the PTO, review them thoroughly and request help from the PTO staff if you need it. The paid services of an attorney well versed in the process would make this job easier. The PTO's current application fee is $325 to file electronically, $375 to file by mail. Forms are available on the website.

Get the wheels in motion early: Approval can take up to two years.

You are probably thinking all this research is overkill for a small fish like you, but it really is worth it. After you have gone to all the trouble and expense of launching your own little labor of love and establishing its name, it would be a major setback to get a cease-and-desist letter in the mail ordering you to stop using that name because it is already federally trademarked by someone else. It would be upsetting and costly to change all your business forms, stationery, literature, and advertising, and website as well as having to explain it to your clients. Do your homework before you christen your "new baby." In the long run, it will be well worth it.

Bedlington and Burrows, Attorneys at Law
1000 Lake Front Avenue
Chicago, IL 60604

February 1, 2011

Mary Ann Smith
Pink Poodle Emporium
200 Garden Grove Road
Wentworth, CA 90970

Dear Ms. Smith:

Your company name (Pink Poodle Emporium) is in violation of trademark infringement against our client, who has legal claim as the sole bearer of this name under the laws of the U.S. Department of Commerce, Patent and Trademark Office.

You are advised to immediately cease and desist using the name Pink Poodle Emporium, striking it from all stationery, literature, and materials in your possession. We expect confirmation of the termination by mail within thirty days of receipt of this letter. Failing to comply with this request will result in costly legal consequences.

Please call us at (312) 555–3456 if you have any questions. Thank you for your cooperation in this matter.

Sincerely,

Edgar T. Bedlington, Esq.

Business Registration Form

State of _____

County/municipality _____

The undersigned hereby certifies that _____ is conducting business under the name _____ which operates as a ___(sole proprietorship, partnership, corporation)___ under the laws of the above-named state.

The business is located at _____(complete street address)_____ ,
_____(suite/room/apt.)_____ , _____(city/state)_____ , _(zip code)_ .

The nature of this _____(product or service)_____ business is
_____(explain fully)_____
_____

The names and addresses of all owners of the above-named business are as follows:

Name

Address (if post office box, also list street address)

_____   _____
_____   _____
_____   _____

The representative of this business declares that the above information is true and correct.

_____

Signature

_____   _____

(print name)   Date

Signed in the presence of:

_____   Witnessed this _____ day of

Signature of witness   _____ , 20 ____

_____

(print name)

Once a name has been chosen, you need to check to determine where you are required to file it to comply with state and local laws. Your accountant and your attorney can advise you on how you should proceed so you will be in full compliance.

In most communities, a person doing business under a name different from his or her own must file a business certificate or "dba" at the city hall or town clerk's office. The only exception to this rule is if you are doing business under your own complete name, such as "The Kathy Salzberg Company." The fee varies from town to town; in my home state, it's around $25 and it's good for four years. Unlike a corporation filing or a trademark, this local registration does not protect your company name. It primarily allows consumers and creditors to identify who you are. The public has a right to know who owns your business. When you open your business account, your bank will also require proof that you have filed your business name with the local authorities.

If you are incorporating your business, you need to file with the Secretary of State's office, under the corporations division. In our state, this requires a $275 filing fee. You do not need to file with the city or town hall if you file with this state office.

Certain partnerships are also required to file at this state level, so it's best to check with your attorney to make sure that you comply. A general partnership, by far the most common type of this setup, would need to file locally, following the same course of action as a sole proprietorship.

The quality of your products and services and the goodwill symbolized by your mark can be valuable commodities and are worthy of protection from infringement by others. A central file listing all trademarks is available in your state's trademarks division office. Once you have started using your trademark, you must register it in your state. This usually costs around $50, and the mark will be registered for ten years, after which it can and should be renewed.

If you are going into business for the long haul, researching your business name and obtaining your own trademark are important steps in protecting the name you seek to establish.

A passion for pet grooming and a head for business don't always go hand in hand. For example, although most people are drawn to grooming because of their love for animals, a 2002 PetGroomer.com survey disclosed the fact that 70 percent of those entering the profession eventually seek to open a grooming business of their own. Interestingly, the vast majority of these business owner wannabes said they never worked with pets and had no previous experience as a business owner.

If you are operating a home-based service business, you might think it is inconceivable that you would need to comply with all the local, state, and federal regulations that apply to commercially located businesses, but unfortunately, this is not the case. The temptation is always there to ignore some rules and regulations, but in the long run, you could be causing yourself problems and stress. Take the time to research the laws that apply to you. Structure your business so that it will be in compliance from day one and you will be in a favorable position to succeed and grow.

Your Mission Statement

Every business needs a mission statement to identify its purpose and its goals. A pet grooming business is no different. It spells out why you chose this business and what you hope to provide for your clientele. It tells people who you are and what you're about.

This statement of your purpose can serve as a source of inspiration for you and your staff. Our mission statement begins with a brief reference to our founder and how his love for pets led him to found this business. It states:

"At the Village Groomer and Pet Supply, our philosophy is to respect that connection between our clients and their humans and to treat every pet in our care as if it were our own. In moments when we are challenged by a nervous pet or a behavioral problem, we try to sense the source of the fear and work with the animal to calm them and make them feel safe. It is our belief that if we always do what is best for the pet, we can't go wrong.

"We strive every day to create a fun, loving, unique experience for pets and their humans. Just come by and see for yourself. The Village Groomer and Pet Supply, celebrating forty-one years of caring for pets . . . and the people they own."

This heartfelt message tells people that first and foremost we are in this business because of our love for animals. It lets them know that we provide a safe place, we have a long history, and we have high standards for the quality of our work. Tap into your own creativity and passion for pet grooming when you compose your mission statement.

If you went into the business because of your love for animals, let your mission statement announce it to the world. If you say you want to be an active part of the animal community, do it. Volunteer to groom shelter pets looking for a new home, help organize and sponsor a pet walk for the humane society, host school field trips to your shop. If you say that your business means more to you than simply a way to make money, you should show it in your actions as well.

Creating a Business Plan

Having a business plan is essential whether you are seeking financial assistance or not. Think of this plan as a road map to help you get where you want to go with your business. Sure, you could still get there without directions, but you would probably take a few wrong turns along the way. A comprehensive business plan outlines the services you plan to provide, your projected cash flow, and your marketing strategy (See sample on pages 31-44). As conditions change in the economy in general and the pet industry in particular, your plan will need periodic updating to keep you on track with regard to your services, pricing, and products as well as how and when you will need to add employees to your staff. It will measure your milestones and track your progress as you become a seasoned veteran in the pet grooming field.

For help on compiling a business plan, you may also turn to that marvelous resource, the Small Business Administration (SBA). With approximately 750 of its

Small Business Development Centers scattered throughout the country, this agency offers assistance free of charge whether you are seeking an SBA loan or going through a bank. To locate an office near you, check out its official website, www.sba.gov. Another great source of help and advice can be found online at www.bizplanit.com.

Why You Need an Attorney

It's time for you to seek professional help. No, we're not questioning your sanity for seeking to enter the crazy world of pet grooming. We just need to point out that a good working relationship with professional advisers—first an attorney, then later an accountant and an insurance agent—will help you organize your business from day one.

An attorney can make sure you comply with all legal and licensing regulations with your business. You probably don't have time to stay up-to-date on the ever changing laws relating to small businesses. You might need help in trademarking your business name. You might need advice on hiring employees, applying for business loans, and entering into contracts. Don't wait until you slip and fall into a legal pothole. Find a lawyer while your business is still in the planning stages.

If you don't know an attorney in your community who specializes in small businesses, ask around. Your friends or other small-business owners may know just the one for you. You could also contact your state bar association, asking for a small-business attorney referral. You may need to meet with a few before you "click" with the right one for you, someone who seems interested and engaged in your plans, an enthusiastic individual who is easy to talk to and knowledgeable about issues concerning your business.

Consider your attorney as a valuable resource, an important member of your team. Be honest and up front about your financial limitations and ask him or her to keep you up to speed on fees as you proceed. It will give you an added sense of security to know that when in doubt, you can pick up the phone and talk to your lawyer. Your attorney will be on your side. He or she wants you to succeed.

When working with animals, there is always a risk involved. Two dogs can get into a knock-down drag-out fight in your reception area. A canine escape artist can make its getaway when you take it out for a potty call. An employee can slip in a puddle. A dog that is severely matted can emerge from your shop with raw, irritated skin needing veterinary attention. A pet whose health is compromised by illness or old age can depart this world when it comes to you for a grooming. Scenarios like this are not pleasant to contemplate, but we all might face them occasionally.

Business Plan for
Fur Magnolias Grooming

402 Maple Lane
Plainfield, MA 02011
(508) 555–8770

Prepared by Jane Smith, Owner
February 23, 2011

Table of Contents

Reasons to Start This Business

I find that I am happiest and most fulfilled when working with animals. I have become adept at grooming my own pets, and for the past two years I have worked on Saturdays and vacations at a nearby grooming shop, helping out and learning the ropes of this business. I started as a bather-brusher and progressed to performing basic clipper trims on various breeds. My employer and her customers have praised my work as I have steadily improved my skills. I now feel I am ready to be on my own and open my own grooming business in my home. The idea of setting my own hours and being my own boss is very appealing to me.

I know I have enough artistic ability to bring out the beauty of each breed entrusted to my care. I have the natural aptitude, and I believe I also have the positive attitude needed to succeed. I am very responsible, dependable, and able to work well with people. I am in good health and have a high energy level, so I know I can handle the physical aspects of this profession. Most of all, I have a deep love of animals and the desire to work with them, making pet ownership more enjoyable for my clients by keeping their pets healthy and beautiful while earning my living in the process.

Credentials

I am now completing a course in pet grooming, which I have been attending on a part-time basis for the past year. Upon graduation, I will receive a diploma stating that I have passed the course and now have the skills needed to groom most breeds of dogs and cats. I will display this formal recognition of my achievement to let my clients know that I am a trained professional.

In my current office job, I have mastered the use of the computer. I have experience in solving customers' problems and explaining complicated information. I will need further training in business management to gain a better understanding of record keeping, taxes, and federal and state laws governing my business. These resources are provided through SCORE, the local Small Business Development Center, and small-business and tax workshops offered periodically by the state and through my local chamber of commerce. Evening courses in business management are also offered at a nearby community college. Plans to strengthen my credentials in this area are listed on the attached Action Plan.

Marketing Plan

I have studied the demographics of my town and the general region and observed that new home construction is on the increase. On average, new homes in this area are selling in the range of $350,000 to $500,000 and are being purchased mainly by upwardly mobile young families drawn to this area because of the growing high-tech industry and our highly rated schools. Most of these newcomers fit the picture of typical suburban family life. Their children are involved in sports and youth groups; the parents own two cars, one of which is often a sport-utility vehicle. The ownership of pets fits right in with this family picture.

The area has also seen an upswing in condo construction, with residents almost evenly split between older empty nesters and younger professionals, both single and married. Many empty nesters find joy in nurturing pets, mainly dogs and cats. They treat their animals as beloved family members and will spend money to keep them healthy and nice to be near. In general, the young marrieds are on the career track, postponing children until they are established. For them, pets serve the role of surrogate children, playing a big part in their enjoyment of leisure time. Many of the condo dwellers do not own dogs but have cats, an easier pet to keep when one works very long hours and travels frequently.

My town has a population of 23,000, with more than 200 service-related businesses. The town clerk's office informed me that there are just less than 2,200 licensed dogs in town. Because cats do not require licensing, I was not able to get a figure on how many residents own cats. However, the population supports one other groomer, four veterinarians, two professional dog trainers, three boarding kennels, one cattery, and two pet sitting and dog walking businesses. I plan to introduce myself to these fellow animal care professionals and give them my business cards as well as requesting their cards to hand out to my clients.

Pet Population Statistics for Potential Customers

I have contacted the town clerks in my hometown and in two neighboring towns and received a list of all licensed dogs and their owners in these communities. The figures will provide me with a database for a mailer announcing the opening of my grooming business.

Promotions

I have volunteered to visit the local high school as part of its career day presentations. With the principal's permission, I will bring my own dog and cat to demonstrate basic grooming techniques. I will also hand out pet grooming pamphlets, featuring my business name and phone number, for students to bring home to their parents. I produced these on my computer using bright-colored paper and clip art of dogs and cats as a border.

I have visited two area animal shelters and volunteered to professionally groom pets that they are seeking to place for adoption, as long as they are current on their vaccinations. The shelter personnel were extremely appreciative, agreeing to hand out my cards to people who adopt pets. Each shelter has its own newsletter, and both plan to highlight my services in upcoming issues.

Advertising

I will inquire about the cost of advertising in the newspapers, one local weekly and one regional weekly as well as two metropolitan dailies. I will also explore advertising in the yellow pages under the "Pets–Grooming" heading and look into advertising in the smaller community phone book, published by a private firm. Radio and television advertisements do not fit into my budget at this time.

My computer software gives me many options to create my own stationery and business cards on quality paper purchased from a local office supply store. My color printer will help make the stationery look more professional. I have already printed sample flyers on my computer to mail directly to potential clients. Business cards will be handed out when I visit area vets, kennels, dog trainers, pet sitters, and shelters. I will investigate the cost of magnetic billboards for my van as well as looking into any potential liability I might incur if I am involved in an accident.

Website

I plan to create a website for my business, initially for promotional purposes but later to feature interactive capabilities. My site will have biographical information and photographs of myself, my pets, and my family. Eventually I will also feature pets from my clientele. I will offer seasonal information on pet safety and links to information on pet bereavement, pet adoption, and various breed rescue organizations, as well as to the website of the American Kennel Club (AKC).

Preliminary research shows that the name "furmagnoliasgrooming.com" is available, and I will register through Register.com, a domain name registry. I wish to protect my Web name, so I will also register under furmagnoliasgrooming.net and furmagnolias grooming.org, so no one else has access to these variations. At present, the cost of each registration is $30 per year. My Internet service provider has web-hosting rates comparable to several other providers, but to conserve my finances, I will look into setting up my Internet site through a free hosting service. My final decision will depend on how my domain name can be displayed and how many other similar businesses are on the server. (I do not want to be at the bottom of a listing of 5,000 sites that takes an unduly long time for the user to load.) Hosting fees start at $15 per month.

I need to investigate the pros and cons of website design as well. According to my preliminary inquiries, website design packages start at $100 for a one-page site. This would have no e-mail or ordering capabilities, but it would secure my site and put my name out on the Internet. I need to look into software packages for website design and the possibility of taking a course in design instruction at the local community college. I know I must weigh the cost factor as well as the demands on my own time as I focus on starting my business. Establishing my website will be irrelevant if no one can find me, so I need to determine how to register it with the most popular search engines, such as Yahoo, AltaVista, and Google. With the explosion of sites on the web, one way to do this would be to register it with Submit-Pro.com, with basic submission fees starting at $20 to connect with 2,000 search engines and directories.

Customer Follow-Up

After I have groomed a pet, I will suggest rebooking it for the next appointment. I may offer a 10 percent discount if one automatically rebooks, at least for the first year or two while I am building my clientele. I could offer special membership cards, entitling these "Preferred Pets" to the discount. This would make the owner feel special, providing a sense of belonging to an exclusive club. I will also call clients a few days ahead to remind them of upcoming appointments.

Pet grooming is offered at two other locations in town: a downtown pet grooming salon and a veterinary hospital. Within 25 miles there are four more grooming shops, plus one obedience training facility with a groomer on staff, one veterinary clinic with a groomer on staff, and one pet supply superstore that offers grooming.

Competitors' Strengths and Weaknesses

Pet grooming salons have the advantage of high visibility and both pedestrian and automobile traffic. On my visits to these groomers, however, I have discovered a few individual weaknesses.

One shop did not look or smell clean, and the owner was equally unkempt and unprofessional in her appearance. Another groomer was abrupt when I visited and introduced myself, possibly viewing me as unwanted competition. She declined to answer any questions about her experience or her pricing. At this establishment, I heard her coworker angrily yelling at a dog in the background, audible in spite of the loud rock and roll music playing on the radio.

The groomers at the pet superstore were friendly, and all were novices to the industry. I liked the open setup that allowed pet owners and shoppers to observe the grooming operation through windows.

At the obedience training school, I was warmly welcomed by the owner. She offered me advice and assistance as well as a tour of her facilities. This was not the case at the vet clinic, where the receptionist told me it was impossible for me to talk to the groomer because he was too busy that day.

These visits showed me that the groomers were busy, highlighting the demand for my service. The varying degrees of courtesy and professionalism with which I was received gave me added incentive to put my best foot forward and make my clients feel welcomed and appreciated. It also brought home the importance of maintaining a bright, clean environment and a warm, friendly manner to make clients feel comfortable about leaving their pets in my care.

My current salary is $36,000 a year, with a savings of $5,000 for emergencies and an untouchable 401(k) plan. Listed here are my monthly salary and approximate expenses to show any monies left over to use for financing my proposed business.

Monthly Income and Expenses

Income

Salary (after taxes and health insurance):	$3,000

Expenses

Mortgage payment:	$750
Food (including takeout):	$300
Car payment:	$300
Gas for car:	$50
Car insurance:	$140
Lunch:	$35
Utilities:	$100
Telephone:	$50
Cable TV:	$45
Cellular phone:	$30
Credit cards:	$150
Laundry and dry cleaning:	$20
Miscellaneous (clothing, toiletries, hairdresser, gifts, pet care):	$100
Recreation (movies, clubs, theater):	$50
Internet fee:	$20
Newspaper and magazines:	$15
Total:	$2,155
Remainder/(deficit):	$845

I will open business checking and savings accounts immediately. I am determined to put at least $500 a month in the savings account to help finance my grooming business.

I will request credit history data from three major credit reporting firms and review the data for discrepancies and repair.

Alternative Money Sources

Bank

My current bank is friendly. Officers and tellers know me well, and I have a long history with this institution. This will make it easier for me to inquire about building reputable credentials to apply for a future loan.

Credit Cards

Two credit cards will be designated for business use only. Charging no more than $300 on each card per month is an affordable limit for me to repay without incurring additional interest charges.

Other Banking Needs

Because clients will expect payment options other than cash or checks, I will inquire about a Visa/MasterCard/Discover merchant account and processing ATM debit. If my bank does not offer merchant accounts, I will need to move my business account to another bank. I will also call American Express to request a merchant application, as this company requires applicants to contact them directly. At the same time, I will request a corporate card for my own use.

Equipment

I already own some grooming equipment (one standard size portable table and one standing floor dryer as well as basic grooming tools purchased through my grooming school). The following list encompasses what would be needed for a home-based grooming salon. Even though I will initially work alone, it makes sense to have space for two grooming stations, as I expect my operation to grow.

For a shop with two grooming stations, I will need the following equipment:

- 2 hydraulic grooming tables
- 2 adjustable grooming posts
- 1 grooming stool (a bar stool would work)
- 2 standing floor dryers
- 1 cage dryer
- 1 high-velocity dryer
- 1 conventional bathtub
- Cages or crates, 6 small and 6 large
- 2 clippers, plus a complete assortment of blades (two in each size) and a set of snap-on comb attachments
- Clipper supplies: blade wash solution, lubricating spray, grease and oil for clipper maintenance

- Scissors, 2 straight, 2 curved for finish work, 1 small straight for feet and ears, 1 blunt tipped for use around eyes, 1 heavy-duty stainless steel for prep work, 1 pair of thinning shears
- 2 universal slicker brushes with curved metal bristles
- 2 stainless steel double-sided combs with both wide and narrow teeth
- 2 mat combs
- 2 dog nail trimmers, 1 large and
- 1 small, pliers type
- 1 cat nail trimmer
- Nailfiles
- 2 pairs of forceps, 1 straight,
- 1 curved, stainless steel
- Ear powder
- 1 nylon muzzle in each size
- 1 plastic "basket" muzzle in each size
- 1 pair of heavy-duty suede animal handler's gloves
- 1 heavy plastic bather's apron

I will need to purchase the following products:

- Shampoos, 1 case (4 gallons) of each of the following types:
  Hypoallergenic, conditioning, medicated (oatmeal and tea tree oil), flea and tick, bluing for white coats, protein-enriched, and all-purpose
- Conditioner, 4 gallons
- Eye drops
- Ear cleaning solution
- Cotton balls or a box of rolled cotton
- First-aid supplies: elasticized gauze bandage rolls, bandages, adhesive tape, instant hot and cold packs, hydrogen peroxide, antibiotic first-aid cream
- Medicated spray to treat "clipper burn"
- Styptic powder
- Wide-spectrum disinfectant to clean grooming tools, tables, crates, and floor
- Flea and tick spray: one type for use on pets who come in with fleas, another to prevent flea infestation in the shop
- 2 groomer's uniforms
- Conditioning sprays: one type to "set" styles, another to combat static electricity in the pet's coat
- Pet cologne, 2 different fragrances
- 1 box of latex gloves

Cleaning Supplies

- Vacuum cleaner (a commercial "shop vac" will work best)
- 1 broom and dustpan
- 1 extra-large trash barrel
- Heavy-duty extra-large trash bags
- Fire extinguisher

Purchasing Plan

I am relying on my contacts in the grooming business to advise me on equipment selection. I know that for this type of business, the least expensive piece of equipment may not be the wisest choice because it must stand up under constant usage. I am researching and reading every book I can find on this subject. Grooming trade shows are held annually in several regions of the country; I plan to attend one of these prior to setting up my shop.

For installation of built-in crates, the bathtub, walls, flooring, electrical outlets, lighting, and a partition between my work area and reception desk, I will need the services of a carpenter, electrician, and plumber. I have friends and family members who work in these trades, so that will help keep the costs of constructing my home grooming shop as low as possible.

How to Start the Business While I'm Working

My employer has asked if I can continue to work two days a week, and I plan to do so while I am building my clientele. The income will help to support me and increase my capital for the new venture. I will have my answering machine take requests for appointments and I will return those calls when I return home in the evening.

Office Setup and Structure

I plan to house my home grooming shop in the "family room" addition off the kitchen that has its own entry. Within this large room, I will partition off a space for use as my office. I have a large closet in which I will install lighting and shelving for storage of supplies.

Business Registration

After researching the federal trademark records to see if the name I have chosen for my business is already in use, I will register my name with state and federal officials. Next, I will request the necessary paperwork from the town clerk and state tax department, fill out the forms and have them notarized, then deliver them for processing.

Mail

Although I have looked into having a separate post office box, for the sake of convenience, I will have my business mail delivered to my home location.

Insurance

General liability insurance for my business must be obtained. According to my current insurance agent, property and liability coverages are extremely limited or excluded in most cases involving home-based businesses.

Other possible sources for insurance coverage may be offered through membership in my local chamber of commerce or the National Dog Groomers Association of America, Inc. I will need coverage for the building, personal property, and liability—extremely important for all persons involved in animal care.

Office Needs

I will use my home computer in my business operation. It includes a word processing program and an inkjet printer. I have a printing program that I can use to make signs and stationery. Initially, I will record clients' names and grooming records on large index cards, but I will look into software programs tailored specifically for the grooming industry.

I will call the telephone company and have another phone line installed for my business. I will also need an answering machine for business use only. Eventually, I may add another line for a fax machine.

I will need a file case for my index cards, and legal pads to record scheduling and grooming instructions for each pet being groomed on a specific day. I will record the date and note the type of grooming I have done on the back of the card. I will also need a daily appointment book and a supply of pens and pencils (entries made in pencil can be easily erased and changed), as well as correction tape or liquid to make changes in my appointment book.

My reception area where I will receive and release customers will be partitioned off from the grooming room. I plan to have a counter installed where my cash register and computer will be kept. Having a separate area will look more clean and professional and keep clients out of my work area.

I will also need a "sandwich board"—style sign listing prices and services.

Expansion

Within one year I anticipate that my business will be generating sufficient revenue for me to hire a bather-brusher. This will make it possible for me to use more of my time in actual grooming, thus increasing my productivity and profit. As with most new businesses, I do not expect to make a profit the first year. The cost of starting up, including training, equipment, remodeling, advertising, and professional services, will take a while to pay off, but I expect to be turning a profit in my second year. I do not think I could expand my staff further at this location because of traffic and parking as well as neighborhood relations.

Action Plan with Completion Dates

Credentials

1. I will graduate from grooming school in January 2011. I will have completed one year's training, which will sharpen the skills I learned while helping out at my former employer's grooming shop and making me more knowledgeable about the proper breed standard for each dog. My diploma posted on the wall will give clients reassurance that I have received professional training.

2. I will further my education by attending trade shows and grooming seminars. (Intergroom in New Jersey in April 2011 and GroomExpo in Pennsylvania, September 2011). If I cannot afford to attend both, I will choose one this year, the other next year.

3. I will immediately request training materials from SCORE, the local Small Business Development Center, and also sign up for any business and tax workshops sponsored by the state. (At this time, my schedule will not allow me to enroll in a course at the community college, but I will have that option when I have left my current job and am working out of my home-based business exclusively.)

Marketing

1. Send mailing to all residents who have licensed dogs in my town announcing the opening of my business (March 2011).

2. Advertise my "Grand Opening" in local and regional weekly newspapers (April 2011).

3. Call the telephone company to place my ad in the yellow pages (January 2011).

4. Call my attorney regarding the use of magnetic signs on my van. If he approves, order the sign (January 2011).

5. Compare web-hosting services and select one to support my Internet site. Also contact website designer and research software to see which course to take in constructing my site (January 2011).

Financial Plan

1. Request personal credit reports from three agencies (immediately).
2. Open business checking and savings account at my current bank or other local bank if mine doesn't offer merchant credit card processing (February 2011).
3. Deposit $500 per month into savings account for business capital (ongoing).
4. Consult with loan officer regarding borrowing options and credential updating (January 2011).
5. Call American Express to request merchant account application (January 2011).

Purchasing Plan

1. Contact distributors in my area to set up credit account and price grooming equipment (January 2011).
2. Contact manufacturers to compare prices and order from the one with the best prices and credit terms. I can also use one of my business credit cards to finance these purchases (January 2011).
3. Buy grooming equipment and supplies after conducting thorough research and planning purchases on a buying chart (first quarter 2011).
4. When products arrive, inspect for damage before installing at shop.

Shop Setup

1. Go to library to check federal records for business name duplication (fourth quarter 2010).
2. Get business registration papers from county and state officials. Complete and return promptly.
3. After inquiring among family and friends, select carpenter, electrician and plumber to convert family room into grooming shop (first quarter 2011).
4. Contact insurance agent to find out coverage needed to take care of my business (first quarter 2011).
5. Purchase telephone with answering machine for business use (February 2011).
6. Contact phone company to make appointment for installation of additional line for business phone (February 2011).
7. Make appointment with health inspector to visit my business (March 2011).

Expansion

1. Review plans regarding hiring an assistant after six months.

Your attorney can advise you on liabilities related specifically to your pet grooming business. He or she should review any release forms having to do with dogs at risk that are left in your care. As pet grooming businesses become more mainstream, they have also come to the attention of federal regulators, notably the Occupational Safety and Health Administration (OSHA). Your lawyer can advise you on safety regulations, record keeping, and training required for employees to make sure you are in compliance with OSHA regulations. (To find out more, log on to OSHA's website at www.osha.gov.)

Because laws regulating businesses vary widely from state to state, your attorney should be consulted to help you meet all of your legal requirements. These will depend on your business structure but may include employment laws, partnership agreements, licenses, reviewing and negotiating contracts, changes in laws and regulations affecting your business, product liability, and protection of your name and trademark.

Business Structure Options

One of the most important areas in this shopping list concerns the legal structure your business will take. That structure will outline control of the business, your legal and financial liability, continuity and transferability of the business, and your tax obligations. The legal structure is the foundation upon which you will build your own little empire, so your attorney's advice is essential in this area.

Once you have chosen a name for your business, the way you proceed will be determined by the type of business structure you plan to set up. The legal structures most small businesses use are the sole proprietorship, the partnership, and the corporation.

Sole Proprietorship

If you intend to be the head honcho, the one in charge of all decisions, you will probably choose the sole proprietorship, whether or not you eventually plan to hire employees. Most home-based businesses are set up under this category. Within the grooming industry, 79 percent of those starting out are sole proprietors. As the name implies, you will be the only owner. For all intents and purposes, you *are* the business. (The one exception to this rule occurs in community property states, where the sole proprietor's spouse is deemed to have a half interest in the business.)

Under a sole proprietorship, the business itself does not pay taxes. Its profits and losses pass over to your personal income tax returns. With you as the sole owner, the business will be set up and funded through your own personal assets and credit sources. Most sole proprietors work alone, but some employ family members or hire help during busy times. This type of business cannot be transferred to another person or handed down to another. If you die, it would cease operation and pass to your estate.

One of the reasons most entrepreneurs choose this form is that it is the easiest way to set up a business. There will be some fees involved in obtaining your business licenses from your local authorities and for your business name registration. The attorney's fees will be less than for other types of business because there is less preparation involved. You do not need to file any applications with government agencies as you would if incorporating. If you have no employees, you won't even need to apply for a federal tax identification number.

The main disadvantage of a sole proprietorship is that the responsibility for everything that happens within the business belongs to you and you alone. As the sole owner, you have unlimited liability in the event of damages, lawsuits, or other financial losses. All of your personal assets (home, car, bank accounts, etc.) are subject to seizure if the business fails. In assessing the risk factors, you need to consider the type of services you plan to provide, the losses that could be incurred, and the extent of your personal assets. It sounds pretty scary, as if you're stepping out on a tightrope without a net, but if you have sufficient capital to see you through the early days, enough insurance to protect you from losses, and sound legal advice, you will probably see it as a risk worth taking. After all, that risk-taker component is part and parcel of the entrepreneurial spirit!

If you plan to hire employees right away, you will need that all-important federal tax identification number. The same is true if you choose to set up under the partnership structure or as a corporation.

Partnership

A partnership is like a sole proprietorship that has two or more owners. There are several variations of this form. The two most common are general and limited partnerships. A general partnership can be formed by a simple oral agreement between two or more persons, but a legal partnership, drawn up with the help of an attorney, is a far better way to go. The drafting of this formal agreement is the major difference in setting up a partnership as opposed to a sole proprietorship. True, it does involve another expenditure for legal services, and you may be asking yourself if that step is really necessary. You and your prospective partner have a trusting relationship and similar goals—what could possibly go wrong? (Happy honeymooners think this way, too.)

The partnership agreement is a tool for handling problems when they crop up. Like what? Let us count the ways. The agreement should cover (a) the type of business you are setting up, (b) the amount invested by each partner, (c) how the profits or losses will be divided, (d) each partner's compensation, (e) the distribution of assets in case the business dissolves, (f) the time limit or duration of the partnership, (g) a dispute settlement clause, (h) restrictions of authority and expenditures, and (i) settlement in case of the death or incapacitation of a partner.

Be smart and get it in writing. Think of it as a prenuptial agreement. With it in place, there will be a reduced risk of misunderstandings about authority, responsibility, control, and the share each party will have regarding profits and losses, depending on what each puts in and takes out of the business. Each partner is legally considered an "agent" of the business and is legally liable for the actions and liabilities of the other partner, so this is not a matter to be taken casually. In some instances, you can be held liable for your partner's activities even if they occur outside the partnership.

If any partners are added in the future, a new agreement must be drawn up. Like the sole proprietorship, the partnership normally requires no government applications, just business licenses.

A partnership really is like a marriage. In fact, many married couples own their businesses as equal legal partners. As in a marriage, before you recite those vows or sign your name on the dotted line, ask yourself if you can work with this person in harmony day in and day out. Do you have unlimited trust in each other's honesty and good judgment? Are you willing to stake your personal assets on his or her actions?

Like a marriage, a partnership offers some advantages. It allows you to start out with more resources and offers more man-hours to devote to the new venture. In setting up a partnership, personal trust and a shared commitment to the success of your new venture are key considerations. It's like a bicycle built for two. It only works well if both riders do the pedaling.

Corporation

A corporation is a legal entity, separate and distinct from its owners. It is the most complex of the business structures we are dealing with and the most costly to organize. It must be chartered to do business by the state in which it is located. Its owners are the stockholders who contribute capital by buying shares in the corporation. They are compensated by dividends, a portion of the corporation's profits. Those with the most shares control the corporation. With control of 51 percent of the stock, a person or group is able to make policy decisions. A corporation's owner can also be an employee and draw a taxable salary.

The stockholders elect a board of directors to run the corporation and act in their interests. In this way, the business owners delegate responsibility and control for day-to-day business operations. Control is exercised through regular meetings of the board of directors as well as annual stockholders' meetings. Strict records and minutes of every meeting must be kept to document all decisions by the board of directors.

The corporation's life is unlimited. If you die, it is easily transferred to another person with no effect on the business (except, perhaps, closing down for the day to give you a proper send-off!).

The major difference between a corporation and a sole proprietorship or partnership is that as a separate entity, the corporation is liable for its debts. While officers and members of the board of directors are responsible for their actions and can be fired or voted out, with few exceptions their responsibility does not extend to risking their personal assets. The stockholders are liable only to the extent of their investment. This limitation on liability is the major reason most businesses become incorporated.

For small businesses, the main disadvantages to incorporating boil down to time, expense, and red tape. To become incorporated, you must draft bylaws, submit articles of incorporation for approval by the state agency that charters corporations, issue capital stock and record its ownership, and pay fees for incorporating that can amount to several hundred dollars.

Once you become incorporated, you must adhere strictly to legal requirements, such as making all decisions through your board of directors, conducting regular meetings of the board as well as annual stockholders' meetings, and filing annual reports with the state. In addition, your tax requirements become more complicated. The corporation itself must pay corporate income taxes on its profits, and the stockholders must pay income taxes on the remaining profits, which are distributed to them in the form of dividends.

One type of corporation, the "S" corporation, presents less of a hassle to the small-business owner. In terms of legal requirements, it is similar to any other corporation, but its profits pass through to stockholders in direct proportion to their number of shares. In this way, it operates more like a partnership. It does not need to pay corporate income taxes. It files tax returns, but they are for informational purposes only. For the small operation, this form offers tax advantages plus the protection of liability not available to the sole proprietor or the partnership. If you are seriously considering incorporating your business, this is an option you should discuss with your attorney and your accountant.

Although sole proprietorships and partnerships present more of a risk to the budding entrepreneur, they continue to be the dominant legal structures for small startups. They present a relatively safe and reasonable option, provided you have done your homework on adhering to zoning laws, having sufficient capital to launch your new venture, securing your business name, and insuring yourself against catastrophic losses and unavoidable injuries. All these provisions plus the training to perform well in your new occupation should put you in a favorable position to start your business. True, you are not launching the *Queen Mary*, but you do need to know your small craft is seaworthy as you set sail on this exciting new voyage.

04 Creating Your Workspace

Now comes the fun part: putting in place the doors and walls, the cosmetic touches, and the shiny new equipment that will give your new business a home of its own. This is where the dream takes shape and becomes a reality. But before you open your doors and invite the world inside, make sure you are in compliance with your local zoning regulations and have taken steps to ensure that your presence will not present a problem to your neighbors.

Are You Zoned for Business?

Your town's zoning officer is one of the first people you should talk to when you are considering a home-based business. In many small towns, this person is the building inspector. Zoning laws are unique to every town and city. They are also subject to interpretation by the local powers that be, so what is allowable in your hometown may not be permitted in mine.

Within each town's zoning bylaws is a chart called the Schedule of Use Regulations. It lists the various zoning districts and spells out in great detail just what is allowed and what is not permitted within each category. The street—or portion of the street—where you live may be zoned as residential only or mixed use (residential and professional or commercial use). The town where our business is located has eleven different zoning districts: three Special Purpose which include Water Protection; Flood Plain; Park, School, Recreation and Conservation; four Residential, including Rural, Residence A for medium to low density single family dwellings, Residence B for medium density single family homes, and General Residence, for low density single and multi-family use as well as public, institutional and recreational use. This one also includes professional offices. Non-Residential Districts include the Business District, Central Business District (the downtown area,) Limited

Manufacturing and the Industrial District. A home office is usually allowed in any residential zone, but you can not assume that it is.

A groomer envisioning a home salon needs to investigate any laws pertaining to the number of persons gathering for the purpose of instruction and the number of vehicles allowed on the premises at any one time. Restrictive parking regulations have put some home-based groomers out of business.

In general, operating a home business within a residential zone in which clients would come to the home for services requires a special permit or a variance from the specified use regulations. In urban or suburban areas, getting such a permit could be a long shot. In rural areas, zoning regulations are not usually as strict. Even if it looks like your plans would conflict with the zoning ordinances, maintain a positive and professional attitude. You may wish to explore your options in seeking a variance or changing the zoning regulations. When you contact your local zoning department, also ask if a home occupation permit is required to do business out of your home.

If your plans would violate the zoning bylaws, find out if there have been similar situations in which a person was successful in obtaining a zoning change or variance. Carefully document the information, getting answers to such questions as: What are the procedures for pursuing such a change? Will I need a lawyer? How long does the process usually take from petition to decision?

Bear in mind that establishing a business is beneficial to the community. As a local merchant, you will be paying taxes at the local, state, and federal level. Document your membership in local business organizations and your current or planned areas of community involvement. Be prepared to discuss issues such as traffic, noise, and good housekeeping.

To obtain a special permit, a hearing would be held before the zoning board. All abutters to your property would be notified so they could attend to be informed of your plans, ask questions, and voice their objections. The board would then take the matter under advisement before issuing its decision. You usually don't need a lawyer at this hearing, but it is wise to have one to present your case properly. You will need legal help as you proceed with your plans, so you might as well involve your attorney in this vital stage of development as well.

If your request is turned down, the zoning board's decision can be appealed in court. Again, you may choose to represent yourself at this juncture, but we would recommend the services of an attorney. Knowledge of the local laws and your options is necessary as you proceed with your plans.

There are many home-based businesses of all stripes that operate without knowledge of the laws governing their existence, but ignorance is not bliss, nor is it an excuse for an illegal operation. The risk involved is not worth it. A written complaint from a disgruntled neighbor or even a business rival can lead directly to a cease-and-desist order, effectively shutting you down.

It would be devastating to invest the time and money in setting up your home-based business only later to discover that you are operating in violation of the law. Finding out the zoning laws of your community is a necessary step in turning your dream into a reality.

Licenses and Permits

Once you have satisfied the zoning requirements and have been issued a special permit—or in some localities, a home occupancy permit—by your local or county zoning department, you will need to find out if a license to do business is also required. Most communities issue such a license for a small fee, usually requiring that it be displayed at your place of business. If the business is to be opened within city limits, the city would issue the license; if outside a city, the county may be the licensing agent. You can find out what is needed by contacting the city, town, or county offices in your area or by going to the SBA website specializing in businesses startups: www.sba.gov/starting/regulations.html. This section offers links to state websites and home pages where the information you need is only a click away.

A Word of Clarification

This license to do business has nothing to do with the type of services you plan to provide. It is simply a stamp of approval that you operate a business. Issuing it also generates tax revenue for your city, town, or county.

Unlike barbers, hairstylists, or day care providers for children, in most states pet grooming professionals are not required to have specific licenses to perform their services. (New Jersey requires that pet groomers become licensed to handle pesticides.) Through industry associations and organizations, however, voluntary accreditation and certification exists in this occupation. You may wish to look into this in the future, as a mark of achievement and to boost your self-confidence.

A groomer who has earned certification or accreditation has completed a course of study and mastered certain skills, passing written examinations and demonstrations of those skills. Having such an official title to feature in your advertising and a certificate to hang on your wall is impressive to your clients and a great source of pride to you. In a 2008 survey by Petgroomer.com, 68 percent of aspiring groomers said they plan to obtain certification.

As pet grooming occupations become more professional and recognized as part of the mainstream, we could see legislation requiring licensing in the future. Pet grooming professionals who have already proven their ability and motivation by obtaining certification or accreditation within their field may have the advantage of being covered by a "grandfather clause" if and when licensing laws do change.

Within the grooming industry, feelings about mandatory licensing are gaining support. A 2008 survey conducted by Petgroomer.com indicated that 91 percent of professional groomers favored vocational licensing. For the time being, licensing requirements remain the subject of heated discussions within the world of pet grooming providers.

Being a Good Neighbor

Once you've gotten your permits and licenses in order, you'll probably feel like heaving a big sigh of relief. You have cleared some hurdles on your path to success, but there may be some other potholes on the road ahead. To be specific: What's the status of your Good Neighbor Policy?

If your pet grooming business will be bringing clients to your home, there could be a potential problem right where you live. If yours is a grooming business, parked cars blocking the street and driveways, increased traffic, dog poop on the sidewalk, or the sound of a roomful of dogs competing to see who can bark the loudest could all spell trouble. A series of irate phone calls to the police department or the board of health could soon close down your business.

To address traffic and parking concerns at your home-based grooming shop, you could stagger drop-off and pickup times so they will not become a problem. To combat problems underfoot, meticulous dedication to keeping your property and the adjacent streets and sidewalks free of dog droppings is an absolute must. Dog feces not only produce unsavory sights and smells, it can also harbor parasites transferable to small children who play in the area. Be vigilant. No matter what the weather, all outdoor areas need to be patrolled and picked up on a daily basis.

After all our years in grooming, it still amazes me that dog owners feel free to let Rover relieve himself outside our front door, then hop in the car and go merrily on their way. One way to address the situation is to have a basket of free plastic "poop bags" on your counter with a little sign telling clients that these are provided for their use—and thanking them for helping you to be a good neighbor. We also have a bag dispenser posted and waste basket outside our entrance as a further friendly reminder.

Noise control can be handled before you open your doors by soundproofing your workspace during the construction process. Because dogs will be on the premises you should also have a big enough area to walk them. Unfortunately, dog attacks continue to make the headlines and the evening news. Although you may not envision such nasty four-legged patrons, your neighbors' fears and their desire to protect themselves and their children must be addressed. Your backyard, or at least part of it, should be fenced.

Your Home Office

So your home-based business is a go. Now where are you going to put your office? Organization should be your watchword here; a pile of papers on the dining room table and a shoebox full of cards in the dresser drawer just won't do. Your office deserves a home of its own.

A spare bedroom, a basement room, a heated garage, or even a section of a room partitioned off with a movable screen could fill the bill. If no extra room is available, it's time to do some serious rearranging. Can you sell or store some furniture to open up some space? Can you do some remodeling to make room for your new base of operation?

Your office will be "command central," the place where you devise strategies, conduct interviews, receive prospective clients, store your records, and set up your computer and phone system. It is the heart of your business from which you connect to the outside world, and so it should be well organized, attractive, and private.

Beyond the highly attractive fact that you don't need to pay rent for this space, there are tangible tax advantages to operating your business from home. Tax laws do change, so it's always a good idea to check with your attorney and/or accountant ahead of time, but in general, the IRS home office rules state that a home office

Action Checklist for Your Business

Completed

1. Choose a name and/or logo for your business, then check at the library and at the secretary of state's office to make sure they are not already trademarked. ❏

2. Make sure all permits are in order. Check with the zoning board and health inspector to determine existing restrictions. Contact a lawyer if you need to schedule a hearing to go before the zoning board for a special permit. ❏

3. Line up your advertising with the the yellow pages and local newspapers. (See chapter 12.) ❏

4. Visit other pet care professionals in your area (veterinarians, kennels, shelters, other groomers, trainers, and pet sitters) to introduce yourself and swap business cards. ❏

5. Apply for a D-U-N-S number from Dun & Bradstreet to help with credit references. (See chapter 10.) ❏

6. Complete the setup of your office area and workspace, including installation of phone, computer lines, and signage. ❏

7. Prepare a complete list of products and equipment you will need to start your business. Research prices on new and used equipment. Visit distributors and order catalogs. ❏

8. Set up accounts with distributors and suppliers for equipment and products needed. ❏

9. As deliveries arrive, check the invoices against your order. Make sure goods and equipment are not damaged. Arrange products on shelves in workspace. ❏

10. Start booking your clients! ❏

deduction is allowable if you use an area in your home exclusively and regularly for business. To obtain current tax information, contact the IRS (800-829-1040; www.irs.gov) to make sure your home office operation falls within specified guidelines.

Drawing the Lines

You are well on your way to establishing your legal boundaries—how about your personal privacy zone? One of the greatest challenges you will face in operating a home-based business is drawing that fine line between your personal and professional lives. If you are a workaholic Type A person, this may mean a struggle to "leave work" and a corresponding lack of private time for yourself and your family. The more laid-back individual might be tempted to take too casual an approach, going in late and leaving early, finding lots of excuses to avoid getting down to business. After all, you're the boss, and every day can be casual day. Your new commute involves stepping across the hall.

In either case, self-discipline is the only answer. In starting your new business, you have chosen a career you love. The workaholic must draw the demarcation line by first installing an answering machine and voice mail. Rule number one: Your personal phone number and your business number are not interchangeable! For the potential slacker, it's time to tone up your work ethic. You need to be relentless about keeping a schedule. You also need to think of your office as a bona fide workplace with its own hours. As far as distractions go, you need to make family and friends aware that even if you're wearing those comfy slippers, you really are at work!

05

By the Numbers: Accounting and Taxes

Becoming a business owner means that you will wear a lot of hats. Being the boss requires a major shift in your mindset. No longer will you look to someone else to tell you what to do. You will always need to focus on the bottom line. When it comes to the roles of manager, employee, public relations specialist, customer service representative, quality control person, financial director, and supervisor, guess what? The buck stops with you!

It sounds intimidating, but to help you plan ahead and sleep nights, professional help from an accountant will prove to be a sound investment as you approach this major transition in your life.

Choosing an Accountant

Unless you are a bookkeeper or an accountant yourself, this is another expert you will need to add to your team. One thing we have noticed about pet grooming professionals in general is that they would rather watch paint dry than delve into the financial aspects of their businesses. Some of the most wonderful animal-care people we know just do not have a head for business. They are so enamored of their profession that they would just as soon ignore the financial side, but as people in the pet grooming industry continue to become legitimate players in the business world, it's time for this to change. The sad fact remains that hundreds of pet grooming businesses fold every year because their owners did not plan ahead and get the expert advice they needed before they joined the ranks of the self-employed. Their dream boats crashed upon the rocks of hard cold reality and financial ignorance.

You may think of yourself as a small potato, but you still need a fully qualified financial professional to help you navigate the waters of taxes, payroll, record keeping, and planning for your future, both personal and professional.

You need someone who specializes in small businesses. Your accountant will help set up your books and obtain the necessary tax identification numbers. He or she will save you time by providing the tax forms you need to file and conform to your legal obligations.

With the ever changing tax laws and the transition to computerization in all things financial, it's important to find an accountant who is up-to-date on current laws and technology. Look for someone who takes advantage of educational seminars, professional publications, and other continuing education opportunities in the field.

You can find an accountant by asking other small-business owners for a recommendation, by looking in the yellow pages, or searching online. You could also ask your attorney or your banker, or contact a state accounting association for a referral. A likely candidate might be found teaching a course at the evening adult education program at your local high school. Interview a few people before you make your choice. You need a person with whom you can communicate well, someone who has the patience and commitment to answer all of your questions, even if you feel silly asking them. (Get over your embarrassment—the only stupid question is the one you don't ask!)

Accounting costs and levels of expertise vary, so don't be shy about requesting fees, credentials, and references. Make sure this is an individual you can trust and that you feel you are being treated with respect. If you find yourself being ignored or feeling like the low man on the totem pole when it comes to information or deadline notification, it's time to find another accountant.

A certified public accountant (CPA) is a person who has passed stringent state tests to obtain a license and a title. This individual can perform audits and issue financial statements. There are public accountants practicing who have not yet gotten their state licenses, and there are certified masters of accountancy (CMA) who have a master's degree in their field. Your accountant should be an enrolled agent (EA), licensed by the IRS to prepare tax returns.

As a cost-cutting strategy, some budding entrepreneurs prefer to employ both an accountant and a bookkeeper. The bookkeeper keeps the books in order and reconciles bank statements, then those materials are delivered to an accountant at tax time. Your accountant should keep you informed about filing quarterly estimated income tax payments, both state and federal, in a timely manner.

Your accountant will work with you to establish accounting and reporting systems, cash projections, tax planning, and financial strategies for the future, serving as your guide through a jungle of red tape. As your business matures, you will call upon your accountant for guidance in helping to meet your financial objectives, seeking assistance with strategic planning, cash management, cost reduction, and management information systems as well as retirement or profit-sharing programs.

Your accountant will format your business information into monthly, quarterly and annual financial statements. Your profit and loss statement will track your income according to bank deposits and list your expenses by category. When the grand total of operating expenses is subtracted from the amount of money gener-ated by your business, you will arrive at your bottom line, the profit or loss incurred by your business for that period. In addition to this record of your income, the accountant will prepare a balance sheet showing your current assets, liabilities, and equity, a general picture of your overall financial health apart from your ongoing cash flow. At year's end, he or she will also prepare an annual financial statement for your business, a valuable tool in helping you to measure your progress and plan ahead. You will want to sit down and go over this data together. Your financial records are open to review by tax authorities, so keeping them up-to-date and accurate is extremely important.

Down the road, complete and orderly financial records will provide you with the data you need if you wish to expand your business, seek a business loan, purchase another piece of property for your business, or make other investments with its financial proceeds. It seems far-fetched at this stage of the game, but if someday you are considering mergers or acquisitions or you need an appraisal to sell your business, you will need to turn to your accountant for expert advice.

If you are seeking a loan, either for startup or for expansion in the future, you will need to have a business plan detailing every aspect of your business to show the bank. (See Creating a Business Plan in chapter 3.) Your accountant will help you with the financial aspects of this plan so you will be fully prepared.

The Importance of Keeping Records

There's much more to running your pet grooming business than grooming furry critters. You need to document every expenditure you make as well as every payment you receive for your services. Each month, these figures will be transferred to your accounting ledger or entered on your computer spreadsheets.

We have heard it said that when you're in business for yourself, your whole life is a write-off. Your accountant and the IRS would adamantly disagree. Even though yours is a home-based operation, it is important to keep your personal and professional accounts separate. To succeed as your own boss, you will need to become a stickler for record keeping.

When you have no one to answer to but yourself, it's easy to get sloppy about the crossover between personal and business expenditures. The good news is that a surprising number of the day-to-day expenses you will incur will indeed be legitimate business deductions. When in doubt, ask your accountant. He or she is paid to keep you on the straight and narrow so you will stay out of trouble with Uncle Sam.

Will You Need a Receipt for That?

The first rule of thumb is always get a receipt. If your job involves driving to service your clients, you need a receipt every time you put gas in your tank. You need all receipts related to automobile maintenance. Keeping your vehicle presentable is also a business expense. Get a receipt when you go to the car wash or have your van detailed. If you pay for parking or pay a toll in the course of business travel, ask for a receipt or push the button dispenser at the toll booth or parking garage and get it yourself.

If you buy stamps for business mailings, including routine bill paying, get a receipt. Every item you buy at the office supply store for your business needs to be tracked with receipts, even if it's just a box of paper clips. Yes, it's always worth the hassle. It's amazing how fast those little expenses add up.

Receipts need to be kept for tuition for courses and seminars you take to develop your business skills; travel and meal expenses when you attend such functions; promotional materials, including greeting cards and holiday cards; uniforms you wear to work; and those T-shirts you had printed with your logo on them. If you hold a staff meeting and get bagels and coffee or pizza and soft drinks for your staff, get a receipt. These are bona fide business meetings.

Your annual party or a business-sponsored trip to the bowling alley or amusement park for your hardworking employees is a legitimate write-off. Your family excursion to Disney World, on the other hand, is not. Check with your accountant about allowable deductions for meals and entertaining. Outlandish expenditures in any category will raise a red flag with the IRS. You need to ensure your actions are completely legal from day one.

If you always put your receipts in the same place, it will do wonders for your record keeping. If your tax returns are ever audited, the IRS will require receipts as proof of business activity. You also need them to track your expenses. Your paper trail will help you to run a profitable business.

Your Balance Sheet

Your balance sheet should be prepared on a monthly basis. It will give you an overall picture of what your business is worth at any given time by documenting your assets (cash, inventory, and equipment), liabilities (whom you owe and how much), and your net worth (the difference between your assets and liabilities). It is an important document to maintain not just for your own knowledge but as part of the financial package that may be needed down the road. Accurate records will be helpful in convincing outside investors and banks of the soundness of your business should you ever seek capital or a business loan for expansion.

The Sample Balance Sheet on page 62 shows how the asset accounts are documented, including accumulated depreciation. Any major piece of equipment you purchase for your business—a computer, a printer, a dryer, or an electric table, for

Balance Sheet   March 31, 2011
Fur Magnolias Grooming

Assets

Cash		$6,670
Accounts receivable		0
Inventory		$500
Office equipment	$800	
Less accumulated depreciation	$80	$720
Grooming equipment	$2,450	
Less accumulated depreciation	$245	$2,205
Total assets		**$10,095**

Liabilities

Accounts payable		$575
Loan payable		$135

Owner's Equity

Jane Smith, capital, March 1, 2011	$6,000	
Net income, June	$1,650	
Subtotal	$7,650	
Less withdrawals	$250	
Jane Smith, capital, March 1, 2011		$7,400
Total liabilities and owner's equity		**$8,110**

Notes

Office equipment:
   printer, $300
   phone, $100
   cash register, $400

example—can be depreciated over a five-year period (sixty months). In the example provided, Fur Magnolias Grooming Salon purchased a printer, a phone, and a cash register for $800, as well as dryers, tubs, and grooming tables for $2,450. Depreciation on the office equipment is $13.33 per month ($800 ÷ 60 months) or $79.98 through June ($13.33 x 6 months), rounded up to $80, the nearest whole number. Depreciation on the grooming equipment amounts to $40.83 per month ($2,450 ÷ 60 months) or $244.98 through June ($40.83 x 6 months), rounded up to $245, the nearest whole dollar. These values would be deducted from your assets.

The owner's equity section shows how a cash withdrawal is deducted from the capital account during the month. It also records the owner's income. But it's only part of the picture. The balance sheet measures the overall health of your business, the assets minus the liabilities. With assets of $10,095 and liabilities of $710, Jane's balance looks pretty healthy. But like all shrewd business owners, she needs to keep a healthy amount in reserve as a financial security blanket.

To determine how much money you will need to spend before turning a profit, it is extremely helpful to document every purchase and expenditure. As a fledgling business owner, this will help you to buy and spend wisely and to prioritize your purchases. The Expense Analysis Spreadsheet on page 64 graphically illustrates how your dollars and cents add up at the end of the month.

Your Income Statement

In running a business, it's not how much you take in, it's how much you keep! Your income statement provides you with this information by detailing the month's total revenue and expenses to arrive at your net income. You can make your income statement as general or as detailed by category as you want it to be. Ultimately, you arrive at your net income after deducting all operating expenses from the revenue your business took in.

Jane's accountant arrives at her monthly bottom line (profit or loss) using a detailed income statement in which every expenditure she made during the month constitutes a line item. For the month of June, Jane made a profit of $2,009.

Cash Flow Projection

A cash flow projection is an estimate of all cash you expect to both earn and spend during a specific period of time. This projection will help you with the delicate balancing act of collecting payment for your products and services and managing your

Expense Analysis Spreadsheet   For the period ending October 31, 2010
Fur Magnolias Grooming

Description	May	June	July	Aug	Sept	Oct	TOTALS
Grooming supplies:							
Shampoos							
Conditioner							
Cologne							
Coat sprays							
Ear cleaner							
Ear powder							
Styptic powder							
Ribbon							
Cotton rolls							
Grooming tools:							
Scissors							
Blades							
Brushes							
Combs and rakes							
Nail trimmers							
Forceps							
Advertising							
Subscriptions							
Telephone							
Office supplies:							
Computer paper							
Printing cartridges							
Envelopes							
Internet access service							
Travel:							
Tolls/parking							
Meals							
Gas							
Hotels							
Bank service charges							
Merchant account fees							
Education							
Computer software							
TOTALS							

Income Statement   For the month ending January 31, 2011

Fur Magnolias Grooming

Revenue

Sales (grooming)	$2,400
Interest earned	$20
Total revenue	**$2,420**

Operating Expenses

Selling expenses:		
Cost of products/supplies	$120	
Advertising	$80	
Total selling expenses		$200
General and administrative expenses:		
Telephone	$48	
Depreciation of office and grooming		
equipment per month	$74	
Other expenses	$89	
Total general and administrative		
expenses		$211
Total operating expenses		**$411**

Net income	**$2,009**

Six-Month Cash Flow Projection

May 2011–October 2011

Fur Magnolias Grooming

	May	June	July	Aug	Sept	Oct	TOTAL
Income:							
Grooming	2,000	3,000	2,500	3,000	3,000	3,000	16,500
Retail	400	500	500	400	400	400	2,600
Total INCOME	**2,400**	**3,500**	**3,000**	**3,400**	**3,400**	**3,400**	**19,100**
Expenses:							
Rent							
Supplies	225	150	125	150	150	125	925
Utilities	75	75	75	75	75	75	450
Telephone	200	200	200	200	200	200	1,200
Advertising	50	50	50	50	50	50	300
Accounting	60	60	60	60	60	60	360
Legal							
Permits and licenses							
Repairs and maintenance					200		200
Laundry	10	10	10	10	10	10	60
Seminars							
Dues and subscriptions		35					35
Office expenses	50	20	20	20	20	20	150
Bank fees	8	8	8	8	8	8	48
Depreciation							
Postage	10	10	10	10	10	10	60
Total EXPENSES	**688**	**618**	**558**	**583**	**783**	**558**	**3,788**
PROFIT	**1,712**	**2,882**	**2,442**	**2,817**	**2,617**	**2,842**	**15,312**

credit before paying your bills—to prevent the dreaded negative cash flow that can result if you do not plan ahead. As you begin your business, anticipating your cash flow involves a lot of guesswork; once you have become established, you will have a better handle on how much you can expect to bring in on a monthly basis, which seasons are busiest, and which ones are usually slower. Then you can plan your expenditures accordingly.

Taxing Issues

Chances are you've been a tax-paying citizen for years, but once you start your own business, you will need to start paying a different set of taxes to both the state and federal governments. These taxes will be determined by the type of business structure you are starting. Let's look at the list of pertinent taxing issues.

Federal Identification Number

If your business is a sole proprietorship with employees, a partnership, or a corporation with or without employees, the first thing you must do is obtain a federal identification number for federal and state tax purposes. This is sometimes referred to as an EIN (Employer Identification Number). To obtain this number, you must file Form SS-4, Application for Employer Identification Number, with the IRS. This form can be downloaded directly from the IRS website at www.irs.gov, or you can call the IRS at (800) 829-4933. Taxpayers can fax the completed Form SS-4 (PDF) application to their state fax number, available on the website of your Secretary of State. (All listed at www.e-secretaryofstate.com). Sole proprietorships without employees are not required to have this federal identification number. Instead, the owners can use their Social Security numbers for business tax purposes.

Sales Taxes

Unless your state does not have a sales tax, if you are going to sell retail products along with your services, you will need to pay a sales tax on these goods to the state. To do this, you must register with the State Department of Revenue as a sales tax vendor, receive a sales tax permit, and file the appropriate returns. You will be legally required to maintain detailed financial records of everything you sell. With very few exceptions, services that you perform—like grooming—are not taxed.

In our state of Massachusetts, we must pay a monthly sales tax of 6.25 percent on everything we sell, with the exception of clothing (for people) valued at less than

$175 per item. T-shirts, hats, and sweatshirts for our human customers fall well below that ceiling, but dog apparel *is* a taxable item. The payment requirements in this state vary with the amount of products you sell. If you collect less than $100 from the sales of goods in a year, you need to file annually. If your sales receipts total between $101 and $1,200, you need to file quarterly. Because we have sales above this figure, we must file monthly, twenty days after the end of the filing period (e.g., February 20 for the month of January). Once you have registered with the state and obtained a password, you may file online at your state's Department of Revenue website.

To avoid paying retail sales taxes on goods that you are buying for resale, you will also need to obtain a resale certificate. You need to be a registered sales/use vendor to get this exemption. Your state website will tell you how to obtain this, or you can phone the customer service bureau at your State Department of Revenue to request the necessary forms. Click on your state to find out about how to conform to sales tax laws that apply to you at www.sba.gov/starting/regulations. html. A more comprehensive guide to all of your state's business tax requirements is also available.

The IRS also offers a publication called *Your Business Tax Kit*, which includes data and forms for obtaining your EIN and a tax guide for small businesses. Call its Forms and Publications Department at (800) 829-3676 or drop by your local IRS office to request a copy.

Income Taxes

Federal income tax is a pay-as-you-go tax. An employee usually has income tax withheld from his or her pay. Our federal government receives 70 percent of its personal income tax revenues this way. As a business owner, you will no longer have an employer to withhold these taxes for you. The responsibility will shift entirely to you. In most cases, you must make quarterly estimated tax payments if you expect to owe at least $1,000 in taxes for the year, after subtracting any credits due and income taxes withheld on your behalf from any sources of employment. Actually, you will probably find that the requirement of paying income taxes on a quarterly basis is a lot less stressful than having to come up with a whole year's tax payment at once. From now on, you will pay both your federal and state taxes on a quarterly basis.

Like all other income-earning individuals, businesses and/or their owners are required to pay taxes on their income. The types of taxes they need to pay and the forms required vary according to the business' structures. If you are a sole proprietor, you are required to file estimated tax payments for income you will draw from your business. Because you and the business are one and the same, this means paying taxes on your profit, or your bottom line. If your accountant is calculating correctly, your quarterly income taxes to both the state and the federal government should provide a pretty close assessment of the annual taxes that will be due, so when April 15 rolls around, you will not be floored by a big tax burden.

You will now need to file the "long form" when paying your annual income tax. In addition to this Form 1040, you will need to file a Schedule C (profit and loss itemization) from your business. Part of this may include a deduction for depreciation on your equipment as well.

Social Security

You will also need to file a Schedule SE (Social Security payments for yourself, which you now need to make as a self-employed taxpayer). If you are a sole proprietor with no employees, your Social Security number will be used when you file your tax documents. Everybody must pay Social Security taxes, but yours will now be made through this Self-Employment Tax. You will need to file Schedule SE quarterly as well.

When you file your annual income tax return, the total of those quarterly Social Security payments you have made previously will be deducted from your final tax assessment. Currently, the self-employment tax rate on net earnings is 15.3 percent (12.4 percent Social Security tax plus 2.9 percent Medicare tax). Quarterly estimated income tax payments for the current year are due April 15, June 15, and September 15, and January 15 of the following year. In our home state, estimated income taxes are also paid on an quarterly basis but the final payment must be paid by December 15 rather than in January. If your state collects income taxes, check with your accountant or Secretary of State's office in case you are faced with such a discrepancy.

If you eventually hire employees, you'll be responsible for withholding federal and state income tax as well as Social Security from their pay. For more information on taxes, see chapter 14, Watching Baby Grow.

There is a wealth of small-business tax information online at the IRS website, www.irs.gov, if you click on "Information for Businesses," then scroll down to "Small Business Products Online Ordering."

Your Taxes Are Your Business

As far as your business income is concerned, the form you use when paying your taxes will depend on its legal structure. Here are some general guidelines:

- If your business has only one owner, it will automatically be considered a sole proprietorship unless you elect to be treated as a corporation. A sole proprietorship files Form 1040, US Individual Income Tax Return, and will include Form 1040, Schedule C, Profit or Loss from Business. As previously stated, your business income is treated as your personal income.

- If your business is an S Corporation, Form 1120, US Corporation Income Tax Return, is filed according to the same deadline as unincorporated companies, by April 15.

- C Corporations must file their annual corporate returns within two and a half months after the close of their fiscal year.

- If your business has two or more owners, it will automatically be considered a partnership. A partnership files Form 1065, US Partnership Return of Income, by April 15.

06

Insuring Your Success

The details of starting your own business may seem daunting, but one area that you should not neglect is insurance coverage. Many different types of insurance exist, including property and casualty, automobile, liability, group health, business interruption, disability income, workers' compensation, and life, including "key man" insurance and others. "You can insure against everything and anything," says Gene Fairbrother, lead small business consultant for the National Association of Self Employed. "The most important thing is to know the risks you are taking."

Property and Casualty Insurance

Your business will need protection from fire, theft, or any other unexpected or uncontrollable losses. If it's a home-based business, the first thing you should do is to contact your insurance agent to find out if riders can be added to your homeowner's policy to cover your new venture. Coverage for a home-based business is not automatically included in a standard homeowner's policy. If your business involves a home office only, ask if your existing homeowner's policy can be updated to include replacement coverage for your office equipment.

When it comes to property and casualty insurance, there are many levels of coverage available. You need to figure out how much money you would need if you had to rebuild or replace your business. This policy would include fire, theft, and loss from weather-related disasters. Working with your insurance agent, you can educate yourself on limitations and/or waivers of coverage. For example, in most states, losses resulting from flooding are not covered in a standard property insurance policy. You need a separate policy or a rider to an existing policy to protect yourself in the event of flood-related damages.

Some insurance companies offer special policies that cover both your home and a business run from your home. Taking this route may be less expensive than adding riders to your homeowner's policy or buying separate policies for home and business. Check the coverage carefully. If you are providing services or manufacturing goods at your home business location, these policies may not be suitable for you.

Automobile Insurance

If you will be using your vehicle as part of your business, as would be the case with a groomer who does pickup and delivery, it will be necessary to obtain auto insurance for any damage or liability that could result during such usage. If you are a mobile groomer, your new business on wheels must be totally insured as well.

Liability Insurance

This type of insurance is usually easy to obtain, but when it comes to pet grooming occupations, liability insurance coverage has been difficult to find. These are relatively new professions with their own unique requirements. Groomers need protection to cover loss of or injury to the animals in their care as well as persons on their premises: pet owners, employees, delivery persons, and visitors. If your insurance agent tells you that no such coverage is available for your business, it's time to go shopping for an insurance broker. An agent works for one insurance company; a broker can select from a wide range of providers to come up with tailor-made coverage for you.

You will need to describe your business operation clearly so that your insurance professional can assess your risks and needs. More and more pet grooming professionals are seeking the equivalent of malpractice insurance in case a pet is injured, lost, or its death occurs while in their care. Until recently, pets were evaluated only as property. What you paid for the puppy at the breeder or the pet store established its dollar value.

However, as the importance of pets to their owners' health and well-being becomes an acknowledged fact in our society, or if your four-legged client happens to be a champion show dog or a working dog, you could end up liable for thousands of dollars in damages if a pet is harmed or lost while under your care.

As a general rule, it is advisable in today's world to have $1 million of liability coverage for your business. It sounds like a huge amount of money, but for the protection and peace of mind you will receive, it really is not that expensive. It will protect you if someone slips and falls on your premises, if a dog jumps off a table and breaks its leg, if a child is bitten, or if a pet escapes and is hit by a car. These are all worst-case scenarios, but Murphy's Law is alive and well, so prepare for the worst, and do everything in your power to make sure it doesn't occur.

We were able to secure $1 million in liability coverage plus all the property protection we need through our agent with the Travelers Group. Because our policy covers a large grooming shop and retail store, it costs more than it would for a small home-based operation, but we pay in monthly installments, making it easier to manage along with our other expenses.

If you find it impossible to get coverage you need, consider going through one of our industry associations. For groomers, such insurance packages are available to members of the National Dog Groomers Association of America (NDGAA) located in Clark, Pennsylvania. Contact them at phone number (724) 962-2711; or e-mail them at ndga@nauticom.net; or go to the website www.nationaldoggroomers.com.

Business Interruption Insurance

Another type of insurance you may wish to obtain is business interruption insurance. Your property insurance policy would pay you to replace damaged or destroyed equipment or buildings, but you would still be required to pay taxes, utilities, and other expenses if your business had to be shut down for repairs. Like disability insurance, this kind of insurance provides you with income when you are unable to earn your living.

Workers' Compensation

If you have three or more employees (counting yourself, unless you are a sole proprietor), you will also need workers' compensation insurance. This type of insurance pays the medical expenses and lost wages of an employee who is injured or becomes ill as a result of his or her job. It actually includes two types of protection: the coverage for employees, plus liability coverage for the employer to pay the cost of defending lawsuits filed by an employee or an employee's family.

Workers' compensation insurance is required by law in all fifty states. Without this coverage, an injured worker could sue your business to recover medical costs, disability costs, and damages. This could effectively put you out of business.

Last year, injuries in the workplace affected thousands of employees and cost US companies nearly $1 billion per week, according to the US Department of Energy. The

number of nonfatal occupational injuries and illnesses reported in 2008 declined to
3.7 million cases, down from 4 million in 2007. Workplace injuries occur in all types
of businesses. The fact is that if you are in business long enough, it is likely that you
will eventually have to deal with a workers' compensation claim.

There are differences among the states as to what types of employees qualify
for benefits, how much coverage a firm must provide, and what percentage of an
injured worker's wages must be paid. Check the regulations for your state either
directly with the Secretary of State's office or through a link provided on the SBA
website at www.sba.gov/starting/regulations.html.

Insurance sales methods for workers' compensation policies also vary from state
to state. A few states require employers to purchase this insurance through a single
state agency; others allow private insurers who sell business insurance to offer
workers' comp policies. Many states also offer "insurance pools" for firms that cannot afford standard coverage, often those with poor safety records or a long history
of workers' comp claims.

If an employee is injured on the job, you must immediately file a claim with your insurance carrier. The carrier will then notify the state department that oversees such claims, and the case will be reviewed to determine whether the claim is valid and what benefits the worker should receive. Usually, employees will not start receiving workers' comp benefits until they have been out of work for five days.

Workers' compensation premiums depend on the nature of your business. Each type of job is assigned a classification code. Riskier work is classified accordingly and charged a higher premium. For a store clerk, you may pay only 48 cents for every $100 in your payroll. Under a specific rate for pet groomers, we are currently $1.12 for every $100 of remuneration.

You may also choose to have a deductible. More than half of the states allow small companies to reduce premiums by paying a deductible on workers' comp claims. Ranging from $100 to $1,000 per claim, deductibles can reduce your premiums, but your costs would be impacted by the number and cost of medical claims filed against you. We do not have a deductible on our workers comp policy because, in the opinion of our insurer, the savings for selecting this option would be minimal and could actually end up costing us more.

Employers are required to post a notice to employees in a suitable place outlining workers' compensation coverage and workers' rights. This is public information and must be readily available to any person who needs it. This official notice, which is available at your state Department of Industrial Accidents (DIA) offices and downloadable from many state websites, must indicate the insurance carrier, the address, the policy number, and a contact person to whom injuries or incidents should be reported. Failure to provide the information to employees is a violation of the law, leaving you, the employer, subject to a fine.

Becoming an informed pet grooming provider and practicing safety in the workplace will help to minimize your risks. When you insure yourself against losses and protect yourself, your employees, and the pets under your supervision through wise business practices, you will be keeping your business healthy as well.

07

As a small-business owner, how should you choose a bank or financial institution? Like the choices of your lawyer and your accountant, selecting the right financial institution and learning how to access its resources can play a major role in your success.

Your Business Bank Account

You will need a business checking account for your pet grooming business. Before you choose the bank that's right for you, it's a good idea to shop around. If you already have a history and a personal rapport with a local bank, that might be a great place to start. It's always good to establish a relationship with a banker before you need money!

It's important to find people you feel comfortable with. As you chat with bank tellers and officers, you will find out if you feel a personal connection. The bank personnel may already know you, but chances are they know precious little about the pet grooming industry. Be prepared to answer their questions knowledgeably. Don't be shy about telling them why your business is unique and letting your enthusiasm show.

Talking to your fellow business associates may also help you make your decision. Your accountant, attorney, and even the local chamber of commerce are all good places to look for a referral. Attend meetings of the chamber or other service organizations to find out which banks are active in your business community.

These days the banking business is more competitive than ever. Sometimes a new bank in the community that is aggressively seeking customers will offer special deals and packages for your business. Bigger is not always better. A smaller bank may give you more personal service and have more relaxed rules when it comes to loan procedures.

Some factors to consider when making your selection are convenience, cost, and the range of services the bank has to offer.

Is it conveniently located? Can you bank by phone or online? When it comes to running your business, time is money. You don't want to waste it by driving a long distance or standing in line for long periods of time while you wait to make your transactions.

Will the bank offer you a line of credit and overdraft protection for your business account? When you need to purchase equipment or launch an advertising campaign, drawing upon a credit line can help you manage your cash flow, and knowing you won't be embarrassed or inconvenienced if one of your checks does not clear will add greatly to your peace of mind.

Does the bank accept federal tax deposits? Will your business be issued its own ATM and credit card? What will the monthly charges be for your account? Can your business checking account have a companion savings account that pays you interest? Can you easily make transfers between the two accounts? (I like to keep money for tax payments in a savings account until such payments are due. I'm collecting a bit of interest on these savings, and it makes me feel more secure to know my tax money is set aside.)

Is there a minimum balance you can maintain to avoid monthly bank fees? In these days of giant bank mergers, some of the larger banks attach charges to everything you do, from using an ATM card to making an online inquiry about your account, even making an after-hours deposit in the lock box. Look for other hidden charges, such as fees for using a teller or writing more than a certain number of checks per month.

Does the bank provide special loan programs for small businesses, including SBA loans or other government-guaranteed loans? Will loan officers walk you through the application process if you decide to seek such a loan?

Although price alone should not be the determining factor in choosing a bank, you should compare interest rates on deposit accounts and basic consumer loans. (Because most business loans are negotiated, rates on these will not be posted.) Don't be afraid to ask for references and ask questions. Bear in mind that you are trying to establish a long-term, mutually beneficial business relationship.

You will turn to your bank for help with cash management, payroll assistance, credit counseling, even investment products. Nowadays banks have their own websites. Check them out to educate yourself on the full range of products they have to offer.

Paper or Plastic? Credit, Charge, and Debit Cards

With consumers increasingly turning to credit and debit cards instead of cash and checks, you should consider accepting credit cards in your business. Many small-business owners shy away from credit card transactions because they don't want to pay handling charges or they think credit card sales are too much of a hassle, but processing plastic has become an everyday fact of life. It's a convenience that will make life easier for your customers and more profitable for you.

Credit Cards

The average American now has four credit cards, up from 3.2 cards in 2004. Credit card usage continues to grow with 14 percent of Americans holding more than ten of them. That's around one in seven Americans, up from ten percent in 2004.

The volume of sales done through these cards has been expanding by 15 percent per year for the past several years, three times faster than the increase in overall purchases in the United States. Around 640 million credit cards are now in circulation with about $800 billion in credit card balances, based upon Federal Reserve figures.

For increasing numbers of American consumers, plastic is the preferred method of payment. Why are credit cards so popular? Let's look at the reasons:

- People don't want to carry cash.
- They wish to avail themselves of rewards, such as airline miles.
- They find it easier to manage their finances by paying one monthly bill.
- They want a record of every purchase.
- They don't want the hassle of providing identification or a phone number and waiting around for verification of a check.

For all the convenience they offer, credit cards are really expensive loans on which consumers pay interest, sometimes up to 26 percent. That interest accounts for 75 percent of the profits earned by banks that issue credit cards. In addition to high interest on unpaid balances, many credit card companies charge an annual fee for their use, late payment penalties, and fees for going over the stated credit limit.

Finally, credit card processing companies profit by charging business owners and service providers a fee for every transaction made by our customers.

Credit cards are processed offline, the purchaser simply signs a charge slip and you, the retailer, have to pay the credit card issuer a percentage of the total purchase, usually somewhere between 1.69 and 3.25 percent. This fee goes to the bank that issued the card.

Charge Cards

Charge cards, such as American Express and Diners Club, also known as travel and entertainment cards, are another popular form of plastic. They differ from credit cards because they have no credit limit. To avoid paying interest, owners of these charge cards must pay off the entire balance when the bill comes in. If charge card owners opt to pay off a large bill over time, the balance can be spread out, but typically they will pay 18 to 21 percent interest, the same rate charged by department stores cards. Charge card companies make their money by collecting big annual fees. They will also charge you, the merchant, a higher percentage for processing when your customers use them to pay for goods or services.

Debit Cards

More recently, debit cards have been added to the mix. In 2006, debit card usage surpassed credit card use for the first time. For 2010, cardholders are on track to conduct 26.6 billion transactions at the point-of-sale, while credit card transactions are projected to be 24.4 billion. Debit card usage at point-of-sale locations grew nearly 23 percent between March 2005 and 2006 while PIN-based transactions at ATMs, the traditional primary point-of-use, actually declined during the same period, further emphasizing the trend that consumers are increasingly using debit to pay for most transactions—including their morning lattes.

What makes debit cards so popular? These potent little pieces of plastic combine the functions of a credit card, an ATM card, and a check all in one.

In addition to their use in ATMs for making deposits, withdrawals, transfers, balance inquiries, and even loan payments, debit cards are now used just about everywhere in place of cash, checks, or credit cards.

The debit card offers all the convenience of credit and charge cards and is far less intrusive and time-consuming than writing a check. Unlike credit and charge cards, a debit card does not use the bank's money. You must have a sufficient amount in

The Pros and Cons of Plastic

Nothing is for nothing, and processing all this plastic comes at a price. The fee charged per credit and charge card transaction varies according to the type of card used and the volume of sales. The transaction fee on cards charged by your processing company (ISO) or individual companies like Discover Card or American Express is called a discount rate and will be itemized on your monthly statement. For a small-business owner whose credit sales total less than $5,000 in charges per month, this rate would usually vary between 1.69 and 3.25 percent per transaction.

Offering credit and debit card sales is a convenience you can offer your clientele and a potential moneymaker for you. Love 'em or hate 'em, credit cards and debit cards are here to stay. By 2007, check and paper credit use fell from 32 to 14 percent of all noncash transactions, a trend that is expected to rise annually.

If your business does retail sales, often people will do more "impulse buying" when they are using a card, especially around the holidays. According to one recent estimate, if you sell retail products, you stand to lose up to 80 percent of consumer impulse buys if you don't accept credit cards. When your business provides this service, it also gives you a certain legitimacy and clout as an up-to-date member of the business community.

There is a downside, however. (Isn't there always?) With the use of credit and charge cards comes the possibility of a "chargeback" if a customer disputes a transaction that appears on his or her monthly bill. Chargebacks can occur when a customer is dissatisfied with merchandise or services, questions the amount of the charge, or in some cases, simply forgets making the transaction.

This dispute leads to a "retrieval," the process of gathering proof that the transaction was indeed a valid one. When one of your customers disputes a charge made by your business, your merchant account number is debited for the funds in question while the transaction is investigated. If you cannot prove the sale was a valid one, the unfavorable result will be a chargeback—or deduction of that sale amount—from your account.

Chargebacks result in a headache involving time and paperwork for the small-business owner, but there are steps you can take to prevent them from happening. Make sure you comply with all transaction requirements issued by the credit card companies, such as checking the cards for signatures, holograms, and expiration dates. If you suspect fraud, call the Voice Authorization Center indicated on your terminal and speak to an operator.

Remember, a sale authorization indicates only the availability of credit at the time of the sale. It does not guarantee that the person presenting the card is the rightful owner, nor does it protect you against chargebacks or credit card fraud.

your checking account to cover every purchase you make when you use it. This built-in discipline keeps users from spending beyond their means.

What are the downsides to debit cards? For the consumer who needs three to four weeks to pay the bills, credit cards and charge cards are preferable. Also, because debit card amounts are removed immediately from the consumer's checking account, the customer does not have the option to withhold payment or cancel a check if a dispute arises over the goods or services paid for. For the merchant, debit cards forestall time-consuming authorizations and the nuisance of bounced checks.

Not all debit cards are created equal. Those bearing the MasterCard or Visa logo can be used worldwide for purchases and ATM transactions. Most issuers do not charge fees for debit card purchases, and the rate charged to merchants for processing them is much lower than that for credit and charge card processing.

Debit card transactions are processed online. Retailers can get those done for a lot less than credit cards and pay as little as 10 cents or so per transaction.

The banks and credit card companies love our customers to use credit cards because they get a percentage of every dollar customers spend. Retailers beg to differ. We prefer that customers choose debit so we don't have to pay those hefty interchange fees.

Debit card transactions are processed for a much smaller fee, usually not more than 50 cents per transaction regardless of the amount spent. From the merchant's standpoint, the risk factor is virtually eliminated. The possibility of credit card fraud or of receiving a bad check is removed, along with the potential loss of revenue, inconvenience, and embarrassment that goes with it.

Opening a Merchant Account

In order to accept credit, charge, and debit cards, you must open a merchant account with a bank. If you are just starting your business, you will need to have your credit reviewed before you are issued this merchant account. If you have no business history, the strength of your credit will depend on your personal credit history.

Not all banks handle credit card transactions, but don't be deterred if your bank does not provide this service. Many farm out their credit card processing to a specialized processor or independent sales company, commonly referred to as an ISO. Whether your bank provides this function directly or you use an ISO, you still need a merchant account to receive credit, charge, and debit card transactions as payment for your goods and services. If this is an in-house function of your bank, its representative will set you up with a data machine and teach you how to use it. You can buy, lease, or rent this machine, with costs varying between $100 and $1,000, depending on your equipment and needs. If you are going through an ISO, its sales representative will handle equipment installation and training. Whichever leasing agent you use, check the length of the lease on the equipment as well as the processing of your sales. We learned this the hard way when we decided to change IPO's to obtain a lower monthly rate. We discovered that we had a three-year contract with the company for processing but a four-year lease on the data machine so we were locked in to pay a monthly fee for an additional year of leasing. Nowadays, it may not be cost-effective to lease the machine at all because you may be able to buy this equipment outright for the same or less than the company's monthly fees.

Corporate Cards

You may also find your own corporate credit card to be a valuable tool in managing your business expenses. The biggest boon in using a corporate card is that it consolidates your bills. If you engage in business-related travel, for example, your company will receive one bill broken down into hotel, rental car, airline tickets, and restaurant costs. Your monthly statement will allow you to analyze your expenses and help you to budget and plan for your business' future.

If you have a partner or a key employee, you may want to consider issuing this person a duplicate corporate card. That person will then have a line of credit in an emergency, and your bookkeeper or accountant will appreciate the record of expenditures your monthly statement will provide. Of course, you would need to review every charge made and make sure the privilege is not being abused by use of the card for personal expenses not related to the business.

Another benefit of using your corporate credit or charge cards may be additional travel insurance. For example, with American Express, you can obtain up to $200,000 in travel accident insurance and $1,250 in baggage insurance to cover lost luggage.

As small businesses continue to blossom all over the landscape, credit card companies are increasingly recognizing their clout. Keep your eyes open for deals and offers that can benefit you and your business as well.

Paper or plastic? We think the choice is clear. The way you handle charge, credit, and debit card sales for your customers and the way you use them yourself to manage your business can make a big difference. They are valuable tools for increasing your success.

08

The Basics of Working at Home

Are you ready to call your own shots? When you are your own CEO working out of your home, it's all up to you. How you design your office, keep track of clients, how high-tech your operation will be, the climate you will provide for your customers—this brand-new universe is yours to create. Blending it seamlessly into your family life may pose a few problems, but you have come this far and are up to the challenge.

Equipping Your Office

Beyond the usual clerical accoutrements—desk, chair, telephone and answering service of some sort, calculator, pens, pencils, paper clips, scissors, ruler, tape, stamps, stapler and staple remover, file folders, hanging files, and labels, you will need the following:

- Schedule book or reservations calendar. The most common one of these is a dated deskpad. From now on, your life will revolve around this item!
- Bookcase and shelves for storing notebooks, computer software, and office supplies as well as your personal library of books and videos on pets and their care. You'll be amazed at how quickly you'll fill it up.
- Filing cabinets for all paperwork, records, and business forms.
- First-aid kit for people and pets.
- Stationery, custom printed with your logo, name, address, and phone number.
- Matching envelopes.
- Plain business-size envelopes.
- Brochures to hand out to prospective clients.

- Notepads with your name and address for writing personal notes to clients.
- Business cards.
- Rubber stamps and inkpad for imprinting checks for bank deposit, return address on correspondence, and pre-addressing invoices for clients' convenience in paying bills.
- A paper shredder. Once you have retired your client forms and records, destroy them before they go out in the trash or recycling pile.
- Accounting ledger. Unless you are using a computer program like Quicken, MYOB, or a similar program, you will use this to furnish your accountant with a monthly report of your financial information. This can be a notebook, a One-Write checkbook system, or a customized software program.

Don't forget to keep a receipt for everything you purchase for your office. It will pay off at tax time.

Client Cards

You will need to maintain a record of every pet that you deal with. This can be a simple index card listing the owner's name, address, and home, business, and cell phone numbers, along with the pet's name, age, breed, sex, and color. You also need the name and phone number of the pet's veterinarian as well as the expiration dates of its vaccinations. It's a bad idea to take pets that have no shot records. You are putting yourself, your employees, and the other pets at risk. It can also make things very complicated with Animal Control if you have to report a bite and you don't have proof of vaccinations. The pet may have to be quarantined and spend time away from its family. It's just not worth the risk. Kennels have been requiring this information for many years, and it's time for all pet grooming businesses to make it a requirement as well.

On your client card you will also need to note any health problems the pet has, such as seizure disorder, heart disease, allergies, hip dysplasia, arthritis, skin problems, or injuries from accidents. For elderly or frail dogs, record that they cannot tolerate certain aspects of the grooming process, like high-pressured forced-air drying. On the reverse side, record special instructions for each visit. For example, a groomer might note "short summer teddy bear clip" or "schnauzer trim, short feathers." Here you might also record the price once the job is done, detailing any extra charges (flea shampoo, dematting, anal glands, etc.).

(front)

Client Card

Last: _____   First: _____   Title: _____

Address: _____

Town: _____   State: _____   Zip: _____

Phones: Home:_____   Work:_____

PhonEmergency:_____   Contact:_____

Comments: _____

Pet name: _____   Breed: _____   Color: _____

D/C: _____   Age: _____   Sex: _____   Weight: _____   CC: _____   Vet: _____

Preferred groomer: _____Schedule: _____ Last: _____ Pending: _____

Remarks: _____

DHLLP   /   /   Rabies   /   /   F/Leukemia   /   /

Bordetella /   /   Lyme   /   /   Corona   /   /

(back)

Client Groomer History

Client: Jones, Duncan   **D/C:** D   **Breed:** Westie

Date: 04/15/11   **Groomer:** Jane
Profile: same
Full groom: $40

Date: 02/02/11   **Groomer:** Jane
Profile: #5 Westie, letting hair grow out a bit
Full groom: $40

Groomer Worksheet

Client: Jones, Duncan

Breed: West Highland Terrier   **D/C:** D   **Sex:** M   **Color:** White

Remarks: Flat rate $40   **Age:** 3

Notes: Barker—out early, rebook 6 wks.   **Schedule:** 6

Profile: #4 on Back, regular Westie trim

Appointment: 02/02/11

Time: 9:00 a.m.

Groomer: Jane   GCD:

Complete Groom	$ _____	Deskunk	$ _____
Handstripping	$ _____	Medicated Bath	$ _____
Flea/Tick Bath	$ _____	Deodorizer Bath	$ _____
Tough Strip Charge	$ _____	Dematting	$ _____
Special Handling	$ _____	Anals	$ _____
Teeth	$ _____		

Groom Profile

Reg. Groom—Blade #_____   Overall/Strip—Blade #_____Other_____

Legs: Scissor_____   Demat_____   Bands_____   Tail_____

Body: Bands_____   Poms_____   Other_____   Ears_____

Face: Cf_____   M _____   G _____   M/G_____

Other Face/Head _____

Feet: Pf_____   Tf_____   Other_____

Collar/Lead: _____

Groomer Remarks:

This is also the place to do your official "check-in" of pets, recording any pertinent information observed at arrival regarding coat condition, health issues, etc. If you notice anything—from an ear infection, to a hole in the coat, to a hot spot—write it all down. Over the years, it is amazing what we have been blamed for as professional groomers. Point out any issues to your client at check in—and make a record! This client card will serve as the pet's history, giving you a record of every visit, the services that were performed, and what the customer was charged.

Computers and You

More and more pet grooming pros are relying on computers in the day-to-day running of their businesses. We encourage start-up groomers to get off on the right paw and invest in a grooming software program. It makes life so much easier.

There many wonderful software programs available to keep track of appointments and client histories. In 1983 Rick Smith of Kennelsoft in Elk Rapids, Michigan, developed one of the earliest versions for groomers, Top Groomer. His company's products have evolved and improved, now featuring the Atlantis software program for managing boarding, grooming, training, retail, and doggy day care as well as the Avalon program, with its grooming salon, doggy day care, and retail management applications. Kennelsoft's customer service is top-notch, and the program is easy to use. Trial versions may be downloaded from www.kennelsoft.com.

Other software systems are available from Dog Days Software (www.dogdays software.com), KennelSuite 7 (www.planesoftware.com), 123 Pet Software (www .123petsoftware.com), and the Groomer's Write Hand (www.groomershand.com).

There are many other software versions available, and you can download demos of them to try before you purchase. Being certain the software is user-friendly is important.

It's all about data. Whether your client histories are maintained on index cards in a file box or in a computer system, you will want to include basic information—the client's name, address, and phone number; pet's name; vet's name and phone number; and health and vaccination information—plus any special notes that will help you in your work.

A grooming software program will let you access your clients' appointments, their pets' particular needs, and their history at a glance. You can easily schedule your services, keep track of pricing and billing, and manage your time far more efficiently once you take advantage of this technology. As your business grows, these programs can also tally commissions for employees with the click of the mouse or keep timecards if you pay an hourly wage. Whether it's your doctor, dentist, pharmacist, pest-control company, or lawn-care service, most personal-service organizations today are managed with the help of a computer. Why should the pet grooming business be any different?

You might want to know when Mrs. Miller last came in with Clancy, her Irish setter. Your client card will tell you that, as well as how much she spent and a brief description of how Clancy was groomed. With a software reservations system, you can find out all that and a lot more. It can tell you how many Irish setters are in your clientele, how many clients rebook on a six-week basis, your history of price increases, the dog's health history, and the idiosyncrasies of that pet as well as those of its owner.

Both systems provide information, but the computer provides a lot more of it a lot faster without the reams of paperwork that have always been part of doing business. A computerized system will give you a lot more information in a lot less time, freeing you up to do what you like best: taking care of your furry customers.

With the right software package, you can schedule appointments and track customers, pets, revenues, employees, and client histories. Most systems also offer accounting packages to track income and produce needed reports. Many of these programs can be exported to Quickbooks, making your bookkeeping much easier at tax time. If your client reservations program does not offer sufficient financial management capabilities, there are several applications that will handle everything from check writing to financial reports. Microsoft Office for Small Business is a leader in this area as is Quickbooks, which will handle all aspects of your data, including checkbook and payroll operations. MYOB offers programs to adapt any small business to computerization. Check out its capabilities at www.MYOB.com.

When considering a software program for your pet grooming business, here are some important questions to consider:

- Does the system offer point-of-sale capabilities if you have a retail operation?
- Is it user-friendly? Can you move easily from field to field and are you comfortable with the program?
- How about customer support? Is it offered 24–7, or must you call within limited hours? Is it free of charge? Are there time limits attached? Will the company help install the software? Will they help train you and your staff?
- How much will it cost? Are upgrades available?
- Do you know anyone who currently uses the system? Ask for their feedback.

Our client files have been maintained by computer for years, and we love the system, but when a client comes in for the first time, we still record the pertinent information on a card before entering data into the computer. These hard copies are kept in a metal card file for peace of mind. We also back up our entire Kennelsoft program once a week onto a flash drive that one of us takes home. If for any reason we were to experience a fire or computer failure, all we would have to do is obtain the software again from the manufacturer and upload our files directly back into the program, so we wouldn't lose a thing.

Invest in a software program right out of the gate. In the long-run, it is one of your most important investments. The time it saves you is invaluable.

The Telephone: Your All-Important First Impression

In any service business, the telephone will be your lifeline to your clients. Most of your business will involve bookings done over the phone.

Clients call to inquire about your services, prices, methods, products, and schedules. Because you will be dealing with their beloved pets, they also want to "feel you out," to get a reading on whether or not you are the type of person they can trust with little Spunky. You may occasionally get phone calls from other pet grooming providers disguising themselves as customers. (It's a dead giveaway when you have to strain to hear over the chorus of barking dogs in the background and the "prospective client" asks the prices on three or four different breeds.) Thankfully, because many of us now have caller ID, that technique of price-shopping is not so common anymore. Besides, you should have a good enough relationship with your colleagues to be able to pick up the phone and ask such a question outright.

Telephone Etiquette and Techniques

Your customer gets a first impression of you and your business over the phone. If you sound rushed and stressed, that client will certainly not feel comfortable and appreciated. If you answer questions as if it's a big bother, he or she will not be encouraged to book your services. Simply put, good telephone techniques reflect common courtesy. Here are some do's and don'ts of phone etiquette:

- When you answer the phone, give your business name and your own name as well. "Good morning, Fur Magnolias Grooming Salon. This is Jane speaking. May I help you?"
- Answer the phone as quickly as you can. People do not like to be kept waiting, and many will hang up after four or five rings. Unless you have caller ID or want to pay for a "star 69" identification, a missed phone call is a lost opportunity.
- Provide all the information you can about your services and your background. Don't just dryly state your prices, explain them. "Yes, that is our price to groom a cat. It can be a tricky process, and it takes lots of patience and skill. If you would prefer, I could sell you the shampoo and the tools you need so you could do it at home." (Most cat owners will gasp at the prospect and book an appointment!)
- Get as much information as you can over the phone. Write it down on your daily desk calendar or begin their customer card in your booking software. This will save time and build an instant bond when the person uses your service.
- Personalize it. "Oh, Jake is a golden retriever. We love that breed. Our family has had four goldens over the years. Aren't they wonderful?"
- Speak in a warm, friendly tone, not in a bored monotone or in a rushed, stressed voice.
- Smile as you speak! The inquiring customer can hear it in your voice. Besides, it's a proven fact that smiling has an immediate physical and physiological impact on you. It increases circulation, lowers your blood pressure,

changes your metabolism, and sends healthy hormones into your system to counteract stress.

■ If you are using an answering machine, personalize your message. It's nice to sound like you love your work and take good care of your clients:

"Good Morning! This is Fur Magnolias Grooming Shop, Jane speaking. I can't take your call at the moment. I am probably up to my elbows in bubbles giving the puppies a bath right now, but if you leave a message, I will return your call as soon as I can. Thanks for your patience, and have a great day!"

■ Do not argue with people who are rude or disrespectful about your policies or prices. ("I never had to get all that shot information from the vet before! Why can't you call him yourself?" or "Forty-five dollars to groom my little Schnauzer? That's outrageous!") Inform them courteously that maybe your service is not the one for them and thank them for calling. When dealing with the public, you are bound to run into some difficult people, but you don't have to allow them push your buttons!

■ Return calls promptly. Potential customers like to feel valued. If they feel ignored, they will shop elsewhere.

■ If you are making reminder calls from your salon, get away from the barking dogs to do so. All that background noise sounds chaotic and unprofessional. People won't want to leave their pampered pooch in what sounds like a doggie insane asylum.

■ If yours is a home-based business, do not let small children answer your business phone. Most folks will not appreciate your toddler's gibberish when they call to make an appointment, no matter how adorable you may find it. If you have older children or teenagers, train them to be courteous if they answer your phone.

Answering Machines

In your absence, we recommend an answering machine over an answering service because you can give the message your personal touch. Clients tend to get annoyed when they reach a person who can only take a message but not answer questions about prices, availability, or services. It is also far more cost-effective to have an answering machine or voice mail system.

As these phone answering systems become more sophisticated, you can also provide a menu option on your machine: "Press 1 if you would like information about our services. Press 2 to change an appointment. Press 3 if you would like us to mail you a brochure. Press 4 if this is a personal call," and so on.

Your personalized message also allows you to add or change information about your office hours, vacation closing, or holiday information. "Happy holidays! You have reached Fur Magnolias Grooming Salon, and we are busier than Santa's elves! We are completely booked until after Christmas, but if you would like to leave your name and a number where you can be reached, we will be glad to put you on our cancellation list. We are taking appointments after January 1, so please leave us a message if you want a return call. Have a great holiday!" (Try to be nonspecific about holidays to accommodate today's diverse population.)

Having "Jingle Bells" or some such festive music playing in the background—softly—adds a nice touch. In any season, instead of the ubiquitous beep, have callers leave their message after a pet sound, a bark or a meow. When you're in the pet grooming business, people delight in humorous little touches like this.

Should You Have a Toll-Free Number?

If you draw clients from a wide area or from across state lines, it may be wise to install a toll-free number. Installation is now easy and affordable, and it's a good selling point for your business. Having a toll-free number that has to do with animals is an added perk. (Our toll-free number is 800–439–PETS.)

All long-distance carriers provide toll-free numbers. Call your provider to ask about their service, rates, and whether those rates fluctuate during the day, evening, or weekends. Also find out if you will have to pay for wrong numbers. (For a while, we got countless calls on our toll-free line for one of the big pet food companies.) Ask how long the service must be in effect and if there are penalties if you decide to cancel before that time is up. Ask about harassment calls. Will they trace such nuisance calls for you? Will you be charged for them?

Having a toll-free number is a great promotional aid in all your advertising—print, Internet, radio, and TV. Keep an eye on your bill to make sure it's cost-effective and that you are not being charged for someone else's calls if your toll-free number was previously used by another business.

Office Hours

If your working hours have always been dictated by somebody else—your boss or the timetable imposed by your nine-to-five job—working from your home will be a huge change for you. You may find that there is always something to distract you from the job, whether it's the demands of family or unexpected interruptions from friends or your own emerging talent for discovering distractions. The weather is gorgeous, and you would much rather go outside and plant some flowers. The mall is beckoning with its siren song of a big clearance sale. It's dark and gloomy today, and you want to pull that comfy quilt up over your head and stay in bed. This is where the need for self-discipline kicks in.

Even though you are working from home, you need to keep regular hours. It's easy to procrastinate—to fix a snack, throw in a load of wash, clean out that hall closet. You need to establish a schedule and to have family and friends recognize that just because you are on the premises does not mean that you are not working. Don't be surprised if things get a little bumpy. When you're just starting out, sometimes your relationship with your significant other will take a backseat and resentment will build up, but you can set aside time for your mate even if it means "penciling in" a special dinner or evening walk after supper.

Sometimes it helps on these special "mini dates" if you limit the shop talk and focus on each other. You want to let your mate know how important his or her support is to you, and you need to use those ordinary everyday moments to nurture your relationship. Neglecting your spouse or special someone can become a habit, so give yourself a priority check from time to time to make sure a failed relationship is not a by-product of your new entrepreneurial zeal.

The telephone can be another huge distraction when you are working at home. You get that sinking feeling in the pit of your stomach when you pick it up and it is your long-lost aunt or garrulous girlfriend about to launch into an hourlong chat. It's not the time or the place, but it's not always easy to disengage. The greatest remedy for this particular problem is that marvelous and inexpensive innovation known as caller ID. Once you clock the time you waste making excuses as to why you can't get into the details of your niece's wedding shower plans or why you don't need another credit card no matter how low the rate is, believe me, this service will pay for itself!

What's more, you now have a business phone. Let your friends know from day one that personal calls should be made to your personal phone number. Leave your home answering machine on and head for your office or your shop. The reverse is true as well. When you are not available to clients, your answering machine will let them know that they can expect a prompt reply.

The Yin and Yang: People-Pleasing and Setting Your Boundaries

Another important skill you will need to develop to keep your work schedule intact is the ability to say no. It's crucial to both your work and your family time. Say no to yourself when you're tempted to raid the refrigerator or watch that TV talk show instead of returning phone calls or doing your paperwork. Learn to say "I'm sorry, but I'm working now" when a neighbor pops in just to chat. Print up a "NOT NOW—I'M WORKING" sign to hang on your office door. When your husband asks you to pick up his dry cleaning during your work time, gently but firmly tell him you can't do it. If you take your job seriously, you will teach others to do so as well. No one can walk all over you unless you lie down!

As you take on this new responsibility, it's important to recognize that there is a difference between being a nice person who takes care of your responsibilities and being a people-pleaser who goes overboard to accommodate others' needs at the expense of your own. Chalk it up to "mother's guilt" or society's conditioning, but this type of approval-seeking behavior is far more common among women than it is in men, and the grooming industry is still more than 80 percent female. The stress of never saying no, of feeling that it's your job to make everything work and keep everybody happy, can take a toll on you physically and emotionally and hinder the success of your business as well.

The Kids Are All Right

One of the reasons you want to start your home-based business is so your schedule will be more flexible. If you have small children, you'll be more available to their needs. This sounds great in theory, but you'll learn that things change every day, and it's not so easy in practice. As you take joy and pride in the fact that your pet grooming business is growing, you'll realize you must master a whole new juggling act.

Most home-based moms try to work around their children's schedules, making appointments in or out of the home when the kids are in school. On weekends, they may rely on their husbands to do the child care while they groom. The work hours and child care coverage you end up with will be unique to your work situation and the needs of your family. The more you can get done when you have built-in child care or when the kids are in preschool or elementary school, the better for you, but there will probably be times when you will need the services of a reliable babysitter. Thankfully, it won't last forever. Paying a sitter can be costly; it's also a great incentive to get as much done as you can when the kids are at school or summer day camp. Once in a while, you may even reward yourself and the kids with an afternoon trip to the playground or the beach. It's good for your own mental health.

As your business grows, those kids will be growing, too, and eventually the child care demands will diminish. They may even end up helping out with the business. In the meantime, try not to become so obsessed with your work that you lose sight of why you made this career switch in the first place. In a business based on personal service, you have the power to schedule your time so that you can get to your son's soccer game or be on hand to take pictures of your daughter and her date as they head for the prom. Years from now, you won't remember that last dog you squeezed in that kept you working late, but you'll never forget those important family moments.

Friendly Relations

When you operate a grooming business, you develop a personal relationship with your clients. This is one of the perks of pet grooming work. You want to be warm and friendly, but there is still a fine line between clients and bosom buddies. Even if you socialize, it's usually wise to maintain certain boundaries between you. Dishing the dirt about your relationship problems or having them unload their true confessions can come back to haunt you. If your client friend later has second thoughts or feels embarrassed about revealing too much, your relationship could suffer, and you could lose business.

If you live and work in a small town, you will also find that when you run to the store for groceries, your clients will usually be in line behind you at the checkout counter. There's no getting away from them, so you always have to be "on," smiling and pleasant even on days when you wish you were on a desert island. When you are a local businessperson, you need to look presentable at all times. Every meeting is a business opportunity. We have booked dogs for grooming in the dentist's office and at a church rummage sale.

If you are driving around town in a vehicle bearing your business name, you can't get caught speeding or losing your temper at someone who just cut you off. You're somebody in your community now, and you must always be aware of the image that you project. Your face may get sore from smiling at all those cute pet stories, but it goes with the territory. After all, folks think of you as a caring person in the extreme, someone who will cherish every little tidbit about Fluffy's daily activities. And you know what? It's good for business!

That personal relationship with clients also kicks in when it comes to your business hours. There is nothing wrong with letting customers know that your family is a top priority with you. "I love my business, but I'm working around my family," says Elaine Belrose of Kibbles & Klips in Blackstone, Massachusetts, whose grooming and boarding business has grown right along with her children "Ninety-nine percent of my clients know this, and they bend their schedules around mine."

Carrie Prest of the Bub'ly Bow Wow in Milbury, Massachusetts, has won more than her share of awards. A professional groomer who has been operating out of her home for more than half of her career, she has been on GroomTeam USA and has won gold and silver medals in Italy and England. Prest groomed at a commercial location for many years. Her life changed drastically after her son's major health problems, and the subsequent birth of two daughters made keeping a daily schedule in the shop all but impossible. Now divorced, she bought a house zoned for business where, with the help of her father, she built her grooming shop in the basement. She says the home-based salon was one of her best decisions.

"You can be there for your children and your clients as well. I have a lot of doctors and nurses who work 7:00 to 3:00, and it's not a big deal to have them drop off their dogs at 6:30 a.m., but my number one concern is people not picking up on time. My clients know that at 6:00 p.m. my doors are locked and I'm with my children."

Diane Betelak of Heads and Tails Professional Grooming in Liverpool, New York, echoes this sentiment. Named American Groomer of the Year in 1997, this international medalist and GroomTeam member recalls the easy convenience of a short walk across the yard to nurse her baby daughter during her first year and later the security of being there when the bus dropped her off from school. "It's the perfect situation for any mother," she says.

09

Constructing Your Home Grooming Shop

Constructing a grooming salon in one's own home is a dream for many grooming profesionals. It's a dream that takes a lot of consideration and planning, as well as a fair amount of start-up capital. You'll be completely renovating an entire area of your home—upgrading its plumbing, electrical, heating, and air-conditioning systems—and furnishing it with grooming equipment such as tubs, tables, clippers, dryers, and cages. In this chapter, let's go ahead and plan your ideal grooming shop. Then we'll deal with the reality of financing your dream—and making the necessary compromises—in chapter 10.

Room to Grow

The space considerations for constructing a home-based grooming salon may be less than those required for a commercial location, but it's wise to give your operation room to grow. Our current grooming space—which is not based in a residential setting—takes up 1,000 square feet and features six grooming stations, two tubs, and crates and cages to accommodate fifty-five pets. In addition to this large room, we have a small soundproofed area for noisy dogs, a laundry/break room, and a restroom. A separate retail area in the front of the shop is equal in size to the grooming room. Guess what? We could use more space! Most of our grooming colleagues would agree. Even if you are starting as a one-groomer operation, you should allow a minimum of 500 square feet for your work area.

A Warm Reception

Once clients come through your door, the reception area is where they get a first impression of your business. It's not all that different from a guest's first visit to your home. Make sure it is well organized, attractive, clean, and spacious enough so that people and their pets will not be tripping over each other, causing congestion and confusion as well as presenting a safety hazard to two- and four-legged customers alike.

Our reception area is not included in the grooming area. Clients are checked in and out at the counter in the front room, the 1,000-square-foot area that also serves as our retail store. The key word is "reception." You want your physical surroundings to convey the same warm welcome you personally strive to communicate to your clients.

Whether you are grooming in a home salon or a commercial space, the requirements are similar. You need to put the same amount of thought into layout and design for both types of grooming businesses. Because of the time and expense involved in creating your salon, chances are you will be living with the results for a long time to come, so plan wisely.

The appearance, atmosphere, and efficiency of your salon layout will speak volumes to your prospective clients. The first thing to keep in mind is that you will be dealing with animals. This is not your doctor's or dentist's office where folks sit quietly and read a magazine while they await their turn. Many of your canine clients will come bounding through the door with their owners in tow. Most are happy and excited to see you and eager to meet and greet each other. Such unbridled exuberance is wonderful, but it's like a kid's birthday party—you need to keep it under control.

Other pets may be timid, hiding behind their owners or trying to fade into the woodwork. They really don't want to be there at all. Perhaps they are experiencing separation anxiety or maybe they're just plain shy, but the last thing these timid canines need is some happy-go-lucky doggie pal jumping all over them, covering their quaking bodies with slobbers and sniffs.

Your reception area should be separate from your work area, which can sometimes be a noisy and hectic place in its own right. Dogs can become very excited when they see people coming and going. There is nothing more difficult or frustrating than trying to groom a pet that is jumping and spinning on the grooming table as it reacts to the presence of an onlooker. It's not a safe situation for pet or groomer. You need to manage traffic flow efficiently, with the comfort and safety of both pets and their owners in mind.

Your desk or countertop where you do client intake should be spacious enough to allow you to wait on a couple of clients at once. We consider safety gates a must.

They should be installed at the entry to your grooming area to keep dogs from either entering or escaping. The entry to our work area features a Dutch door, the top and bottom of which open independently into the groom room. The top half of this door has a Plexiglas window, allowing clients to see into the groom room. If we are working on a hyperactive or unruly pet or if an owner arrives early to pick up a dog still on the grooming table, both portions of the door can be closed, and a shade can be drawn for the groomer's peace of mind and the dog's protection.

Your front desk or counter should be roomy enough to feature some display materials and a few impulse items—dog cookies, flea and tick collars, and promotional materials and brochures. If you plan to sell collars, leashes, toys, and treats, these should be displayed nearby on pegboard or in bins. Fancy gift items like ceramic dishes and pet-related art objects are best displayed in well-lit glass cases, keeping them free from pet hair and dust, unending by-products of your grooming operation. Ask any groomer: Pet hair ends up in the darndest places, from ceiling fixtures to your undies!

The need for client seating is debatable. Some groomers like to offer a regular waiting room, complete with comfortable couches and refreshments like bottled water, coffee, and tea. Your reception area should have room for your computer terminal, phone, cash register, adding machine, electronic credit card machine, and filing systems. You can store office supplies and some retail items under the counter or in a nearby storage closet. Like the floor of your grooming area, the reception area floor should be an easy-to-maintain, nonslippery vinyl surface. Ceramic tiles are too expensive, and, like pebbled or distressed linoleum surfaces, tile grouting is too hard to keep clean. As for carpeting, forget it. Except for a mat by the front door to wipe muddy feet and paws on stormy days, rugs have no place in a grooming salon.

Room to Groom

Your grooming area also needs a smooth, nonslippery floor. Rolled vinyl works best. A light color on both the floor and the walls brightens the room. When you are grooming, you need all the light you can get! Fluorescent overhead lighting fixtures that provide illumination as close to daylight as possible should be located directly over each grooming station. We use 8-foot warm fluorescent bulbs hung in pairs lengthwise and crosswise over our grooming tables. Check with your local power supply company, which may offer incentives to upgrade to more eco-friendly lighting. Some salons add spot lamps to better illuminate each groomer's work station and eliminate shadows. If you have windows, don't cover them up. Natural light is good for both pets and people, but you will probably need blinds to keep the sun from shining directly on the groomer's work area at certain times of day.

Starting out, you will need two grooming tables. Hydraulic tables work best, allowing the groomer to raise and lower the table to accommodate each dog as well as rotating to reach each area of the pet as they work. Tables should be standard size, 24 by 36 inches. They are usually priced from $450 up.

When it comes to handling large dogs, nothing beats an electric table. These are larger, usually with 24-by-42-inch tabletops. Their most impressive feature is that they lower to around 12 inches, allowing the bigger dogs to step right on. They can be raised as high as the groomer needs to work comfortably, safely holding up to 250 pounds. They range in price from around $750 to $1,500. This may seem like a hefty investment when you're starting out, but bear in mind the fact that groomers make more money on large dogs, and lifting them is hazardous to your back. Shop around, and check manufacturers' warranties.

Rubber "fatigue mats" at each grooming station will make standing much more tolerable. Another item to make this labor-intensive job easier on the body is a stool. Many groomers like to sit while doing their job, a skill not everyone can master, but one that makes this career a lot easier on the body. A simple bar stool will do, with or without a back support, but if you want something more ergonomic, check out beauty supply companies and price the stools they provide for the hairstyling industry.

Tools of the Trade

When it comes to grooming, time is money; organization of your tools and your workspace is key. Each groomer needs his or her own workstation. If you went to grooming school, you probably graduated with your own "kit," a toolbox full of supplies needed to do your job. Most schools estimate that you need to spend between $1,000 and $1,500 for the tools necessary to begin your career.

Now that you have your own shop, you don't need to lug this tackle box around anymore. Get yourself a high-quality plastic caddy on wheels with its own drawers to store tools and supplies, or have shelving built and pegboard hung so everything you need is within easy reach. Caddies are available from grooming equipment manufacturers like Petlift or Edemco and the PetEdge catalog (www.petedge.com). For a lot less money, the ones you find in the household goods department of the major discount stores can also be adapted to fit your needs.

Some groomers like to install mirrors, giving the grooming station the look of a human beauty salon. Take some field trips to other grooming shops and, if possible, attend seminars on shop design at industry trade shows to familiarize yourself with various design options for your grooming stations.

On top of your rolling cart you will want to keep items you will use for each grooming: liquid ear cleaner, ear powder, styptic powder to stop bleeding if you nick a dog's nail, coat sprays, and cotton balls. A favorite cost-cutting solution for keeping a supply of cotton on hand is to purchase it in boxed rolls at a beauty supply store. Handy little items like nail files, nail trimmers, elastics for bows, tweezers, stripping knives, and first-aid supplies can be kept in the caddy drawers, along with brushes, combs, and mat-splitting tools. Protective devices such as muzzles and animal handling gloves as well as larger rakes and shedding blades can be hung on pegboard at your grooming station.

Each groomer will need two clippers and two sets of blades of every size. A backup clipper is needed in case you run into mechanical difficulties with one. Having blade duplicates will allow you to send one set out for sharpening and still do business. You will also need the full spectrum of snap-on comb attachments, a great time-saver for today's groomers. Supplies for maintaining your clippers are also important. You will need blade wash solution, lubricating spray, grease, or oil, and an old toothbrush for cleaning blades. If you employ other groomers, they will probably bring their own tools, now the norm for grooming professionals. For bather-brushers and grooming assistants, providing the tools of the trade would be your responsibility as the shop owner.

As an artist working on a living canvas, your scissors are the paintbrushes you use to create your masterpieces each and every day. You will need a 9- or 10-inch heavy-duty pair for "roughing," the prep work you do prior to the bath. These scissors are wider than your finishing shears and sometimes referred to as "88-style." You also need two straight and two curved 8 1/2-inch scissors for your fine finish work; two pairs of blending shears for debulking and shaping; one pair of blunt-tipped scissors for work around the face or fanny; and a smaller pair (5 1/2 to 6 1/2 inches) of straight shears to trim ears and footpads. Optional items include 10-inch straight or curved shears, great time-savers when working on big scissoring jobs like sheepdogs or standard poodles.

Scissors come in a wide price range, but you do get what you pay for. Carbon steel is durable, holding a good edge, but it can rust if you don't keep it dry and oiled. Stainless steel, sometimes combined with chromium or other metals, is rust-resistant. Ice-tempered steel has been subjected to subzero temperatures, changing the metal so it becomes much harder and holds an edge longer.

Blade edges differ as well. Honed and razor edges are so sharp they leave no marks when you use them on a pet's coat. Serrated edges have tiny grooves to hold the hair as they cut. Hollow blades are ground inside to reduce their weight and provide a smooth cut. Like major-league baseball players with their bats, every groomer has certain preferences about how scissors should feel and perform. Because each pair differs widely as to weight and tension, it's best to try it before you buy it, sampling the scissor displays offered at grooming trade shows and conventions or visiting a grooming supply house.

Be good to your scissors and clippers and they will be good to you. Don't leave your precious and expensive equipment on the grooming table where it can be dropped or kicked to the floor. Place your scissors and clippers out of harm's way. You can get a hanging organizer or a leather holster for your shears, with built-in pockets for each pair. When you put your scissors away, don't just stick them in the drawer with their edges unprotected. Store them in their own individual cases. Pamper your clippers as well. Learn the basics of clipper maintenance—cleaning, lubricating, replacing brushes—and make it part of your weekly routine.

Holding Patterns

Crates or cages to hold pets waiting to be groomed, sitting under a dryer, or ready for their owners to pick them up are best arranged against the walls of your grooming shop. For safety reasons, they should be in full view as you work. Some dogs get stressed in cages and try to dig or chew their way out, injuring their noses, mouths, or paws. Nervous pets sometimes urinate or defecate in their crates—usually after the bath, of course! Pets also need to be closely observed during the drying process. Heat stroke is a groomer's worst nightmare; unfortunately, some dogs have succumbed to it at grooming shops.

Cages and crates are available in many styles and sizes. Multi-cage units usually feature six to nine spaces of varying size, stacked in three tiers. Some multi units come on wheels, making it easier to clean your shop and rearrange your system. Stainless-steel cages with removable floor pans and wire racks are expensive, but they can be cleaned and disinfected easily, and they last for decades. Fiberglass cages are another alternative. With them you can design your own stackable units.

Besides being easy to clean, this material comes in pretty colors and is highly resistant to germs, stains, and odors. The major cage and crate manufacturers—Clark, Snyder, Petlift, and Edemco—will help you plan your salon and meet your needs in this important part of your overall design.

You can also custom-build your own stacked units using individual wire cages placed inside homemade wooden frames that can be painted with washable enamel in bright colors. In our shop, in addition to multi-cage stacked units, we use custom-built crates that resemble stalls, better described as "cubbies," designed with Formica floors for easy cleaning. Stacked in two tiers, the bottom rows offer larger units for dogs like Labs and German shepherds, with smaller ones for dogs like poodles and schnauzers on top. Dogs are secured in their cubbies by vinyl-coated cables attached to hooks on the back wall. For dogs that panic when confined to a cage, these cubbies offer a great alternative, and they were relatively inexpensive to install. Are you lucky enough to have a carpenter in the family?

Pipe Down!

Right up there with pet hair, noise is another by-product of a busy grooming operation. Your neighbors will definitely not want to hear dogs howling, yapping, and barking every day. You can reduce noise levels by installing sound-absorbing ceiling tiles when you build your shop. Our grooming room features a soundproof cubby area, visible through glass sliding doors, for the very vocal members of our canine clientele. Noise is stressful for the groomer and the other pets as well. Schedule your little yippers to get them in and out as quickly as possible, cutting down your own stress level and helping to keep peace in the neighborhood while you're at it.

Plug It In

When planning and constructing a grooming salon, the need for electricity is a major consideration. Think about all the things that require electricity: lighting, clippers, dryers, heating, air-conditioning, computers, vacuum cleaners, air purifiers, and even your radio, coffeepot, or a microwave oven. They all call for "juice" and lots of it. You will need an electrician to help determine the number of outlets you will need and where they should be placed.

When consulting with your electrician, you will also need to examine the load requirements of all your equipment to make sure your electrical panel can handle it without blowing fuses or tripping circuit breakers. Will standard plugs do the job, or will you need special 20-amp outlets for heavy-duty dryers and air-conditioners? Upgrading your electrical panel can be a costly proposition, so do it right when you design your salon to avoid expensive alterations down the road.

Keeping It Cool

One of the biggest draws on your electricity will be your air-conditioning system. In the grooming shop, it is absolutely necessary for the comfort and safety of yourself, your coworkers, and the pets in your care. Keep in mind that expired dog breath is 102 degrees at 100 percent humidity! The air in the grooming shop gets real hot, real fast. Even in New England, our air-conditioning unit is operating nine months out of the year. Every day there is a duel between the hot air of the dryers and the cool air of the AC.

How can you reduce the load? It stands to reason that the less time your dryers are operating, the less hot air they will be producing. Never put sopping wet dogs in a cage or a crate to dry. Towel or force-dry them first until they are merely damp, not dripping. Change your air-conditioner filters often. Pet hair clogs up everything in a shop, from air-conditioning filters to computers! Use exhaust fans in your tub area. Consider augmenting your array of dryers with newer units that re-circulate room-temperature air rather than using heating elements. In warm weather, turn all dryers to the "cool" setting. Consult with an air-conditioning contractor as you plan your shop to make sure your system will operate as efficiently as possible.

In the grooming shop, the bathing and grooming areas heat up the fastest, but you need to air-condition your entire shop, including the reception and retail areas. Yes, it is expensive to install it and pay those monthly utility bills, but it's essential for the professional groomer. Learn from our mistakes: we've have had to upgrade the air-conditioning system in the latest salon three times to bring it up to speed, with a considerable cost outlay each time. Bite the bullet and build it in from day one. You'll save yourself money and headaches down the road.

Fluff and Buff: Dryers for Your Salon

There are three types of dryers to consider when outfitting your grooming salon.

Standing Floor Dryers

You will need two standing floor dryers for finish and fluff drying your canine and feline clients. These are the workhorses of the grooming industry, used for blow-drying pets on the table or as they sit in a cage or crate. Their prices usually reflect the amount of power they have to offer; you need to determine how many amps they will take to operate. Heavy-duty ones may require a 20-amp plug and receptacle; most will use the regular 15-amp service.

Generally, it's advisable to have a heavy-duty high-velocity model for thick-coated dogs as well as one that produces an average flow of air for the smaller breeds and cats. Some stand dryers deliver a variable airflow, between 107 and 250 cubic feet per minute (CFM), giving you the option to adjust the power according to the size and coat of the animal being dried. Stand dryers range in price from around $250 to $800, and different manufacturers offer different warranties.

We shy away from plastic housing on dryers because it tends to break easily if the machine gets tipped. Because these dryers are top-heavy, some tip more easily than others, another factor to consider when making your selection. The dryer stand should be sturdily constructed with well-balanced legs on casters that roll freely and can be cleaned easily of that pesky substance that gums up everything in no time: pet hair!

A standing dryer should have a long arm with an adjustable nozzle that can rotate to 360 degrees to direct the airflow in any direction. It should also be adjustable for height. Shop your shows and ask any veteran groomers you know what works for them. Buying a "bargain" dryer that doesn't hold up can be an expensive mistake.

Safety Note

If used properly, cage dryers are safe. They become unsafe if they are used in poorly ventilated areas or if dogs are left under them too long. The potential for heat prostration exists for any dog that is not closely monitored under the dryer, especially those who are elderly; have health issues such as heart, trachea, or lung problems; or those whose breathing may be compromised by very short muzzles, like pugs or Pekingese. Your safest bet is to get one with an automatic timer or one that recycles room-temperature air, requiring no heating element.

Cage Dryers

Cage dryers are a boon in a busy shop. They clip on to the front of the cage or crate to blow-dry the pet. Some have temperature-selection knobs and timers that alert the groomer when the pet has been dried long enough. I use an "octopus" dryer with three hoses that blow warm air to three cages at once. This multi-cage unit does not have a heating element, eliminating the danger of "cooking" a dog.

Cage dryers are relatively inexpensive, ranging in price from $140 to $400. Some manufacturers now offer a dual-purpose stand dryer with a hose attachment for cage drying. Used properly, cage dryers will increase the efficiency of your grooming operation.

Force Dryers

One of the greatest innovations in the grooming industry has been the arrival of the force dryer. This high-velocity dryer uses a nozzle that sweeps excess moisture from the coat, usually while the dog is still in the tub. As the airflow is directed at the coat, the water blows off the hair shaft, drying the coat without brushing. The animal still needs to be dried for finishing, either in the crate or on the table, but the time required is enormously reduced, cutting down on your electric bill in the process. In our shop, two such 20-amp dryers are placed next to the tubs; each can generate 45,000 feet per minute (FPM) of air speed.

Although force dryers have greatly improved grooming speed and efficiency, they are not without drawbacks. Manufacturers are starting to produce quieter models, but most are still quite noisy. In addition, some sensitive pets cannot tolerate their "wind tunnel" effect. For this reason, they should never be used full-force on small, elderly, nervous, or aggressive dogs, nor should they be used at full power on cats. On all pets, one should avoid using their powerful airflow on faces, ears, or genitals. Put yourself in the pet's place: You probably wouldn't find this a pleasant experience either! Towel-dry these sensitive areas of the pet's anatomy instead.

There is a right way and a wrong way to use force dryers. If used improperly on long-coated breeds, their powerful airflow can actually tangle and mat the coat. For such dogs, use the force dryer hose without its nozzle, sweeping the hair in one direction only. Otherwise, you may find yourself spending twice as much time, having to demat the dog both before and after the bath.

Force dryers vary greatly in price, from the small "vacuum cleaner" model that starts around $100 to the 20-amp box units priced around $600.

Splish Splash

Many modern shops separate the "befores" from the "afters" when it comes to canine customers. Keeping unbathed pets in a separate area prevents them from soiling clean pets or passing on fleas or ticks. If you cannot do this in your workspace, at least have one area for dogs who come in with parasites or have been sprayed by a skunk, keeping them away from other pets.

Place your bathing area near the back of your salon—the more self-contained, the better. Keeping this vital component of your operation separate reduces noise and heat in both your reception area and your main grooming room. When adapting your space to accommodate your home grooming shop, have a vent installed in the bathing area to get rid of excess hot air and humidity. An exhaust fan can draw it out through the roof or an exterior wall. This also helps to cut down on the demand for air-conditioning.

If you can provide a grooming table next to the tub, prebath brushouts can be performed there, cutting down on those piles of dirty hair rolling around like tumbleweeds in your main grooming area. This table will also be a great help for force-drying pets before they go into a cage or crate for additional blow-drying.

Ideally, you should have two bathtubs: one standard size for most pets, and a smaller one (the size of a laundry sink) for cats and small dogs. We have used porcelain and fiberglass tubs, but we made the switch to stainless steel, which can be cleaned and disinfected easily. The new tubs are self-contained units that have their own backsplash panels and foldable ramps to help bathers get the big dogs in and out of the tub. Each one has a specially installed hair trap to prevent clogged pipes. Hair and soap can combine to jam up your system, creating a potentially huge expense and inconvenience, and possibly affecting the entire neighborhood as well!

Inside each tub are vinyl-coated racks to keep pets from standing in soapy water as they are being rinsed, which speeds up the drying process. Unless you buy such self-contained units, you will need the services of a carpenter to frame and build a support system for your tubs.

The Plumber's Friend

Consult with a plumber as you plan. The closer you can place your bathing area to existing water pipes, the less costly it will be. Plumbing work can quickly become very expensive. If we were constructing our dream salon from scratch today, we would include a floor drain to accommodate spills and save the floor from water damage.

Grooming uses lots of water, much of it hot. Today's automatic bathing systems, such as the Bath Pro 5.1 by Jarden Consumer Solutions, aid greatly in water conservation and help cut down on water bills. A standard-size forty-gallon water heater may be adequate if yours is a small operation. In our salon, we require a seventy-five-gallon heater to keep us in hot water all day long.

Your bathing area should be tiled or walled with plastic or fiberglass panels. Tubs should be installed at waist level, eliminating unnecessary bending for the bather. You will need shelving for shampoos, conditioners, and towels as well. Like your grooming area, the bathing area needs to be well lit and well maintained for the safety and well-being of workers and pets alike. Spills must be mopped up as soon as they occur. Pets must not be left unattended in a tub. Safety practices really boil down to good common sense, but it's important to make them part of your routine from the day you open your doors to your first customer.

Incidentals

Every grooming salon needs basic supplies like waste containers, trash bags, paper towel dispensers, a shop vacuum cleaner (preferably one that can be used for wet and dry cleanup), fire extinguishers, smoke detectors, locked cabinets for storing toxic cleaning supplies and pesticides, brooms, dustpans, mops, pooper-scoopers, light bulbs, extension cords, and a basic tool kit including a hammer, pliers, and screwdrivers.

You will also need a first-aid kit for people and pets. Check out the OSHA regulations and make sure yours is in compliance.

Nothing makes owners happier than a pretty bow on their freshly groomed pet. A ribbon rack will help organize and manage this decorative little item. Save yourself a bundle by learning how to make your own bows.

When Nature Calls

Your salon will also need a restroom for you and your future employees—nothing elaborate, just a toilet, sink, medicine cabinet, and storage for paper products and cleaning supplies. The needs of your furry customers are another matter.

Like it or not, your clients will inevitably allow their furry friends to relieve themselves on and around your property. If only you could install a pet porta potty! A special "potty walk" area is the next best thing. It will make life a lot easier for all concerned. Include a small signpost to let owners know where to walk their pets. On the counter in your reception area, offer a basket of plastic "poop bags" for clients to use, and station a trash can in the potty walk area. Check out www.dogbag.com, the site for Doggy Walk Bags. They have a display dispenser with signage just for this issue.

Even with all this encouragement, some folks just will not pick up after their pets or confine their elimination to a designated area. You must be extra vigilant to do "potty patrol" each and every day. Dog waste is unsightly and can be harmful to your health. Urine stains buildings, kills grass and plants, and smells awful. To maintain your property and keep good relations with your neighbors, keep your potty walk clean. In addition to your daily pickups, wash it down with a sterilizing agent at least once a week.

Read Any Good Books Lately?

Here's a nifty little area that won't bust your bankroll: your own personal grooming library. Start off with just one shelf. You will need a place for those wonderful reference books that no groomer should be without. First and foremost, you should have the AKC's *Complete Dog Book*. This all-time best-selling dog book offers the official standard for every breed within the AKC's registration. It also contains a wealth of information on breeding, health issues, training, registry, and events within the world of dogs, a wonderful sourcebook for the serious pet grooming professional.

Other important books for your grooming library include *From Problems to Profits: The Madson Management System for Pet Grooming Businesses* by Madeline Bright Ogle, *The Stone Guide to Dog Grooming for All Breeds* by Ben and Pearl Stone, *The All Breed Dog Grooming Guide* by Sam Kohl, *The Complete Poodle Clipping and Grooming Book* by Shirlee Kalstone, and *Notes from the Grooming Table* by Melissa Verplank. We treasure the monumental *Atlas of Dog Breeds of the World* by Bonnie Wilcox and Chris Walkowicz. Two delightful and informative books by Myrna M. Milani, D.V.M.—*The Body Language and Emotions of Dogs* and *The Body Language and Emotions of Cats*—are fantastic for gaining an understanding of the animals we care for every day. A comprehensive book on first aid is also a must.

Having your own personal library is important to your sense of pride in what you do. You may also wish to stock some videos on grooming the various breeds. Having a TV and VCR or DVD player would be another item to add to your wish list. You can learn to groom each breed from some of the industry's most accomplished groomers, such as Sarah Hawkes, Jodi Murphy or Sue Zecco and Jay Scruggs in the privacy of your home or shop.

Dress for Success

When we first started grooming back in the 1970s, most of us wore jeans and T-shirts to work. At that time groomers' uniforms consisted of nylon smocks that could have doubled as maternity wear. No more! Today's groomers can pick and choose from a wide variety of stylish uniforms that are highly attractive and practical, too. In wash-and-wear fabrics that repel pet hair and look sharp, they are another indication of our newfound professional pride.

One of the best things about being a groomer is that you can kiss the power suit, pantyhose, and high heels goodbye. Men, you can ditch the buttoned-down shirt, pinstripe suit, and, best of all, the necktie! However, that does not give us permission to look sloppy. Ripped jeans that fit like you were poured into them, T-shirts with X-rated slogans, bare midriffs, halter tops, short shorts, coffee-stained sweats, and tons of jewelry or long dangly earrings are no-nos. Your personal style is an indication of your pride and professionalism. The clothes you wear tell others who you are. They can serve to enhance your image or detract from it.

Uniform manufacturers are always present at industry shows and conventions to show off their latest fashions, and their products are surprisingly inexpensive. Contact Stylist Wear in Garland, Texas, at (800) 288-9327 or www.stylistwear.com. For the pet stylist fashionista, check out the new line by Jodi Murphy (www.jodimurphy.net). Major distributors also carry groomers' uniforms. Dress for success in your grooming career, proudly portraying the image of a professional in the community.

Oodles of Options

While we're at it, let's include a sound system to serenade yourself and your furry clients with the soothing sounds of classical, New Age, soft rock, or smooth jazz—no raucous rock or rap, please! It's hazardous to the stress levels of both humans *and* animals.

There are countless options when it comes to equipping your dream salon. You probably won't include them right away if you are keeping your eye on your bank account, but isn't it fun to dream? Eventually you may want to add an automatic shampoo system with a central pump dispenser or tanks to deliver the shampoo of your choice right to the pet's coat in the tub, cutting down considerably on the waste and spillage that can occur when you pour from bottles.

Our wish list includes an air purifier system to improve the quality of air for pets and humans alike and to alleviate odor problems. A dehumidifier placed in the bathing area would also cut down on moisture and temperature, allowing dryers to do their job more efficiently.

While we're on the topic of air quality and your health, a vacuum attachment for your clippers, such as the one made by Clipper-Vac, will remove most of the hair from the air you breathe as you clip dogs. Groomers ingest hair and pet dander every single day, another occupational hazard. This device would be a worthwhile investment in your health and longevity in the grooming profession.

A central vacuum cleaner system is also a good idea—no clunky canister to trip over, and instant cleanliness at the flick of a switch! One of our innovative fellow groomers had her husband rig up a homemade version, installing a commercial vacuum in the basement with an extralong hose attachment accessible through wall vents in her salon.

An emergency generator like the ones used by veterinary hospitals is another item on our wish list. Can you think of a more frustrating situation than having the power go out in midclip or finding yourself surrounded by a roomful of wet dogs that can't be dried? Murphy's Law applies everywhere, including the grooming shop.

If you have the room and the resources, consider adding separate laundry facilities for your grooming business. Our salon also features an employee break room, with a coffeemaker, microwave, and a small refrigerator. Having a place to sit and eat your lunch out of the hairy environs of the grooming salon is a dream come true. We also placed a picnic table in the outside area in back of the shop so employees can take a well-deserved break in the fresh air in warm weather.

It's hard to admit, but many grooming shops of yesteryear were sweatshops, dingy places where everything in sight wore a fuzzy coat of dog hair. Thankfully, as the industry has come of age, that image is fading away. Pet owners will no longer settle for second-rate when it comes to caring for their beloved pets. Today, our shops vary widely in character and design, but they do reflect our pride in the grooming profession. As a home groomer, your workplace will be where you live. That's the best reason of all to plan it wisely, make it efficient and attractive, and keep it clean as a whistle!

10 | Financing Your Grooming Business

Do your homework before you begin the process of constructing and equipping your grooming salon. You'll want the most bang for your buck, but you'll need room to grow and quality equipment that will stand up to heavy use. If you are on a tight budget like most budding entrepreneurs, you'll probably be living with your choices for a long time!

What Will It Cost?

Okay, now for the reality check and the compromises. What will your dream grooming shop cost? When it comes to estimating the cost of starting a home-based grooming business, there are countless variables. First of all, there is remodeling the space your operation will use. Construction costs will vary according to what you need and will be different for every budding home groomer. The cost will also depend on what hired professionals will charge—carpenters, plumbers, electricians—as opposed to labor provided by you, your family, and friends. One word of caution: Unless your cousin or your neighbor is a licensed plumber or electrician, to satisfy the building inspector you will need the services of these pros.

If you are adding on to a structure, of course you will need a building permit. As far as carpentry, painting, and floor installation go, a do-it-yourself project can save you a bundle. Whether located at home or in a commercial setting, grooming operations usually need to upgrade the capacity of their building's electrical, air-conditioning, and heating systems. You will need a separate water heater. In a commercial location, the landlord often shares in leasehold improvement costs, but at home, you're on your own.

Either way, remodeling and system upgrades could cost as much as $15,000 to $20,000. You'll want to plan very carefully, determining what you absolutely need to start with and what can wait until later. And you'll want to take advantage of all the "free" family labor you can get! Of course, rather than start your grooming business in a home-based shop, you can choose to begin in a mobile grooming van. For more information on mobile grooming, including the costs, pros, and cons, see "Taking Your Show on the Road: Mobile Grooming," on page 123 of this chapter.

And then there's the equipment. It's easy to go overboard when purchasing equipment for a new salon. Pardon us for dragging out that old chestnut, "Rome wasn't built in a day." You could blow all your cash on state-of-the-art stuff for the shop of your dreams and quickly find yourself out of money. Stick to your business plan and begin with the essentials. As your business and your bottom line grow, you will be able to make those special purchases to improve your salon without jeopardizing your solvency in the process.

The basic cost of equipping a salon with two tubs (one large, one small) and two grooming stations is between $6,000 and $10,000, depending on the amenities you provide. Again, just stick to the basics, like folding tables and tubs from your local Lowe's or Home Depot. Hydraulics and stainless steel tubs will come as your business grows. This estimate does not include a computer or other office equipment and supplies, nor does it include the costs of licensing and advertising. Most importantly, it does not include the cost of supporting yourself while the business is being built.

So what will you need for your office and reception area, if they will be one and the same? A desk and chair, a phone with an answering machine, a cash register, stationery, and office supplies ranging from rubber stamps to a calculator are bare-bones essentials. Your final cost will be affected by variables such as whether you already own a personal computer and printer you can use for your business as well as whether you plan to purchase software, a fax machine, shredder, and copier. The estimated cost of equipping your office can vary between $1,500 and $3,000.

Many home groomers don't give up their "day jobs" for a while, working part-time at something else while they are building their clientele. The sad statistic regarding new businesses is that half of them fail within the first four years. The main reason they go belly-up is undercapitalization. Again, your best tool for ensuring your success is a good business plan. This document outlines your resources, projects your cash flow, and helps you set goals so you can make decisions based on reality, not wishful thinking. Of course, if you are seeking a bank loan to start your business, you will need your business plan tucked under your arm when you go to meet the loan officer. Even if you do not plan to seek outside financing, your business plan will be an important management tool in making every business-related decision you will face.

Business experts tell us that it's generally advisable to have enough cash on hand to take yourself and your business through one full cycle, typically one year. One of the good things about grooming is that our typical clients come in at four- to eight-week intervals, providing us with a great turnover rate. Rebooking those clients is absolutely essential to the health of your operation.

The Importance of Rebooking

In the early years, a lot of our dogs were once-a-year clients—big, furry outdoor dogs who got clipped down every spring. "Once a year, whether they need it or not," we used to joke. Thankfully, in most locations, times have changed. Dogs have moved inside, and their owners like them to look and smell nice. Our animals are family members, and people are getting accustomed to the pleasures of sharing their homes with a well-groomed pet.

There is also science that shows us that six weeks is a perfect rebooking schedule for dogs. Why? Canine skin is made up of several cellular layers. On average it takes six weeks from the time new cells develop at the base until they move up through the layers and reach the top of the skin, where they ultimately die and slough off the dog. This is the dead skin we see when we brush a dog. It make sense, then, to bathe a dog every six weeks and wash away the dead skin cells.

Longhaired breeds and mixes should never be allowed to "winter over" in a mass of matted hair. Not only are they unsightly and smelly, but when they get wet, it can take days for them to dry, leaving them susceptible to chills and illnesses. Encourage these pet owners to be "seasonal" visitors on a three-month schedule if they aren't open to a six week schedule. And remember, if you strip a dog with a #10 blade every time they visit, they won't need to come back for many months. Leaving a little more coat on a dog keeps them cuter and keeps your docket full! Your people skills will be called into play as you recommend rebooking to your clients. As a professional pet grooming provider, it's up to you to educate them about how often their pets should be professionally groomed.

Shop Till You Drop: Where to Buy It

As you plan your equipment purchases, it would be wise to review industry trade magazines such as *Grooming Business Magazine, Pet Product News, Pet Age, Groomer to Groomer,* and *Pet Business* as well as the catalogs of major suppliers, all of which offer online shopping. Among the top distributors are Pet Edge of Beverly, Massachusetts (www.petedge.com); Ryan's Pet Supplies, Phoenix, Arizona (www.ryanspet.com); Jeffers Pet, Dothan, Alabama (www.jefferspet.com); American Pet Pro Wholesale Grooming Supplies, Hayward, California (www.americanpetpro.com); LNC Pet Supply, Sun Valley, California (www.lncpetsupply.com); LDC Professional Pet Products, Waukesha, Wisconsin (www.a1petsupply.com); and Petfood Warehouse, East Rockaway, New York (www.pfwh.com).

These are national companies, but there are hundreds of smaller vendors and distributors that serve a regional clientele. These are the folks who will fill your weekly orders for shampoo, flea and tick collars, brushes, and combs. The majority of all major distributors will ship your order to your door. Ask about shipping minimums or buying levels that will avoid shipping charges altogether. Again, fellow groomers will be a good source of recommendations on where to buy supplies.

A website listing all major vendors and manufacturers can be found at www.petgroomer.com. This comprehensive website also features thousands of pages of grooming information, plus calendar listings for upcoming regional, national, and international grooming conferences and trade shows. These events offer a great opportunity to equip your salon while pumping up your motivation in the process. Some of the major equipment manufacturers like Petlift and Edemco sometimes offer seminars on salon design at these shows. Their reps are always available to answer your questions and assist you in the planning process.

Subscriptions to magazines like *Grooming Business Magazine* and *Groomer to Groomer* are provided free to professional groomers. They often feature articles on salon design and management, grooming products, and the latest equipment trends. Last but definitely not least, before you shop, pick the brains of those who have gone before you, people who make their living in the grooming profession. Arm yourself with knowledge before you whip out that checkbook or credit card!

Obtaining Credit with Wholesalers

When you go shopping to equip your salon, you will usually need to pay up front for grooming equipment—tubs, tables, dryers, clippers, etc. Unless you already have a personal relationship with these folks, your initial transactions will be paid for with cash or a credit card. Once your business is up and running, you can obtain credit for purchases, with the balance to be paid according to the distributor's terms—within ten, fifteen, or thirty days. This is standard practice for items you intend to sell as retail goods to your clients. You buy them wholesale, usually double the price for your retail, then pay the distributor according to the terms agreed upon. Dog food has less of a mark up, usually at 28 to 30 percent, but certainly worth considering if you want repeat retail business. As you are starting out, you will need to build a relationship first, beginning with a small credit balance that will be increased once you have proven to be a reliable customer. Your first few orders for flea collars and dog biscuits, for example, will probably be C.O.D. or paid for by credit card. After a few such orders, call the company and ask if you can establish an account. This means they will ship merchandise to you without payment, then bill you according to the terms they've stated.

The distributors will most likely have you fill out a credit application. If they ask for a credit reference sheet, provide this information on your own letterhead. At this stage, you might never have heard of such a thing, but if you have a D-U-N-S number, include that, too. Dun & Bradstreet, an information services firm that provides business information to companies that make marketing, insurance, or other credit-related decisions, issues this number at no charge. You can register your business by contacting Dun & Bradstreet and answering a series of general business questions regarding ownership, projected revenues, and business history. Why bother? A Dun & Bradstreet number will allow you to register for certain business-related events. It will also give you clout when you go looking for additional credit. To find out more, call Dun & Bradstreet at (800) 333-0505 or apply online at www.dnb.com.

If you do not have any business references to list on your credit application or credit reference sheet, use personal references. A company likes to see five or six references listed to verify your creditworthiness, but if you can provide only three or four, do so. If you are turned down, explain to the distributor that you intend to purchase products often and ask if there is any other way an account can be opened. If you are told to reapply in the future, then it's up to you to prove yourself by paying your bills on time before you come back to ask for credit again. Remember to conduct yourself like a businessperson. Don't take rejection personally. Everybody was the new kid on the block at some point in time, and if you maintain your winning attitude, you will eventually get what you want.

FUR MAGNOLIAS GROOMING

Credit Reference Sheet

D-U-N-S No. 22-333-4444

Bank

Prosperity National Bank

1415 Main Street

Plainfield, MA 02011

(508) 555–1500

Checking Account #09-123456-0

Credit References

Peterson's Pet Products

899 Jefferson Boulevard

Clarkville, MA 02789

(508) 555–9876

Account #604115

Dodson's Doggie Duds

44 Bridge Road

Springdale, MA 02033

(782) 555–1317

Account #123777

Fido's Factory

85 Rolling Terrace

Southport, RI 00543

(401) 555–0099

Account #25-888

Sunshine Pet Shampoos

88 Bridge Road

Eastview, MA 02077

(781) 555–1122

Account #566791

Leo's Leather Leads, Ltd.

2345 Lariat Lane

Sunset Pines, TX 80910

(603) 555–0099

Account #157-903

402 Maple Lane, Plainfield, MA 02011

Telephone (508) 555–8770

Managing Credit to Your Advantage

If you succeed in obtaining credit, make sure you understand the terms. Is there a minimum purchase or a special price for quantity buying? What is the company's return policy? How do you receive credit for damaged or missing items in an order? What if you are disappointed in a product? Can you return it for an exchange, a credit, or a refund?

Some vendors offer discounts if you pay by a certain date, usually 4 to 10 percent off the total cost. These are special terms, usually reserved for repeat customers.

Once you have established a relationship, your distributors can be your best friends. Sometimes they will give you special terms on a major purchase—an electric table, for instance. They may allow you to pay it off in three monthly payments. This is because you are now a known commodity. As a startup, you don't have this sort of mutual relationship . . . yet.

Why do they make it so tough? Unfortunately, many distributors and vendors in the pet grooming field have been burned. Many people start their pet grooming businesses with very little knowledge of how a business should operate. They fly by the seat of their pants, hoping for the best, then they crash and burn, leaving their creditors holding the bag. Don't be one of them. Use your credit wisely and responsibly. It's one of the best things you can do for your professional reputation and the future of your business.

You should also obtain an American Express corporate card for business use. Through OPEN Network, its small business network, you can obtain a line of credit for you to use to manage your cash flow, allowing you to stock up on inventory, buy a new piece of equipment, or make needed improvements as your business grows. This is a very flexible credit line for the small-business owner in good standing, and it's a whole lot easier than going to the bank for a loan. It allows repayment in installments instead of when the monthly bill arrives. The OPEN Network also offers business advice, information, and savings through its network partners. Contact American Express Small Business Services to find out more. Check their website at www.americanexpress.com and click on "Small Business."

To Sell or Not to Sell?

We firmly believe that you should have basic retail items in your salon. When little Fluffy and Max come in to get groomed, their devoted owners often think about buying a treat to reward their pets or a new collar and leash to dress up their glamorous doggies. Their shopping lists may include flea and tick products, poop bags, dental health and breath items, ID tags, chew toys, stain and odor removers, lint brushes, ear and eye cleaners, vitamins, nail clippers, and brushes and combs to maintain those pets between appointments. You can add substantially to your income with impulse items like these.

Why send your clients elsewhere to find these products? Why listen to their pet problems every day, suggest solutions, and then send them down the street? As a pet grooming professional, you carry a high degree of credibility with these clients. After all, they entrust you with the care of their beloved pets. In providing these retail products, you are helping them to take better care of their animals. You are acting as a problem-solver for them. Learn to listen for cues in conversations with your clients and recognize them as sales opportunities. Tell them about a product, lead them to it, and put it in their hands as you explain how it will help them. Don't be shy! Adopt a businesslike perspective. You are not taking advantage of these folks; you are helping them and making a profit in the process.

Of course, if you decide to sell goods, you will need to keep track of your sales taxes. Most states have a sales tax, and you need to register with your state's Department of Corporations and Taxation to receive your sales tax number. See chapter 5 for more information on collecting and paying sales taxes.

Ask and You Shall Receive: How Your Distributors Can Help You

If you do opt to sell pet products, there are ways around spending big bucks on displays. Many distributors that deal primarily with treats and toys offer displays with minimum orders. We have rarely spent money on displays in our 1,000-square-foot retail area, yet our displays are always fresh and attractive. How do we do it? We make deals! Just like us, all of those good folks out there selling products are trying to make a profit, so make them work for you. It's a win-win situation!

Let's eavesdrop on a couple of typical conversations we have with sales reps:

"I see your product doesn't come with a display, but I know I can get a display from this other company. I just really wanted to do business with you because I've heard so many good things about your company."

"I'll buy the deal, but you have to throw in a display, and I'll only feature your product in the display. That means I *have* to buy from you again, right?"

Develop relationships with your sales reps. Being in business is all about interacting successfully with people. A nice display sells more, so you'll make more money, and so will they! And after you have an established relationship, when you are reordering, don't be shy about asking for a better price. Make them work for you, because if they won't, someone else will.

Buying in Bulk and Product Storage

It's in your best interest to become a wheeler-dealer. That's part of the fun of being in business! You can get some great deals when you buy products in bulk, whether it's flea collars or gallons of shampoo. The case price always beats the individual price. Of course, you will need a place to store these bargains. Remember as you design your salon that you can never have too much storage space.

If the products you are purchasing by the bushel are edibles, long-term storage could also present a problem. Even dog biscuits have a shelf life. They can get moldy or attract moths if stored too long, so what appears to be a big bargain might not turn out that way. Learn to read product codes, especially if you plan to sell pet food and snacks.

Date codes for shelf life on dry pet food, cookies, and snacks are pretty straightforward, stating the product is "best sold by" a particular date. Canned goods are another matter. Each company does it differently, some clearly indicating an expiration date, others using numbers indicating the code of the plant where it was produced, the number of the batch, and the number of the day (from 1 to 365) and

Never Pay Retail!

One of the best things about being in business is that when it comes to business purchases, you don't have to pay retail. When buying products from a company that sells retail as well as wholesale, all you have to do is provide your state tax ID number and you can avoid paying sales taxes on your own purchases. Suppliers are sticklers for this tax ID number, so be sure to have it handy. The success of your business is measured by profit margins. To win at this game, you should try to squeeze every penny you can out of every purchase, keeping your eye on that all-important bottom line.

year when it will be out of code. In case of a recall, these numbers would identify the product. The pet food company sales representative should inform you about these codes when you agree to sell that product line.

Inventory Control

If you have chosen to do some retail, you will need to keep track of your inventory. When that consists of a dozen flea collars, some cookie treats, and slicker brushes, it's pretty simple. But as the number of products you carry grows—and sells—you will need to know what you have in stock so you can keep up with customer demand and not lose valuable sales because you don't have an item in stock.

To keep an accurate count and make sure you are getting what you pay for, inventory items should be examined and counted as you unpack the boxes. By law, a count of your inventory is required once a year for tax purposes. You will need to provide it to your accountant. For insurance purposes, you also need to document the value of everything you have in stock as well as your grooming and office equipment. Keep a list of every product you sell and record the quantity on hand for accurate record keeping. Your inventory's value is a combination of each item's cost plus any shipping charges you paid.

Here is an example:

12 flea collars	@ $4.50	=	$54.00
12 flea powders	@ $3.50	=	$42.00
12 flea combs	@ $1.00	=	$12.00
	Subtotal		$108.00
	Shipping		$9.00
	Total cost		$117.00

The cost of shipping ($9.00) divided by the total number of products shipped (36) equals 25 cents. You would add this 25 cents to each product to get the true cost for your inventory as well as to arrive at the price you will decide to sell it for.

Some people like to keep their inventory on a spreadsheet to document each product, the quantity available, wholesale price, and quantity sold to date. Others use software programs such as Mind Your Own Business (MYOB) or Quickbooks. We utilize a point-of-sale system with a bar code scanner just like the supermarket. Among the many features this system provides is an inventory tracking system that produces a weekly order for each vendor and tracks our profits as well. Although it may seem to be too early for a purchase like this, keep it in mind for when your business grows.

Taking Your Show on the Road: Mobile Grooming

Another worthwhile option for the groomer who wants to operate out of his or her home is mobile grooming. This segment of the business has really come of age, growing from 4,000 mobile groomers in 2000 to 10,000 in 2010. With today's demand for convenience and individual service, there is plenty of room for the mobile groomer. Many pet owners, including the elderly and those with disabilities, have trouble transporting Fido to the grooming salon. For them, having a grooming shop on wheels roll right into the driveway to provide care for their pets is just what the doctor ordered.

Once again, you need to do your homework. Some cities, towns, and counties require a license or permit for a mobile business, and some neighborhood or condominium associations may not permit commercial vehicles to be kept at your home. Once you have completed your training, all you need to go mobile is a fully outfitted van. They come in many sizes and models, from brand-new custom-built units to converted RVs or trailers. They can be extremely attractive and luxurious, featuring state-of-the-art grooming equipment such as clipper vacuum systems, hydraulic or electric tables, dryers, ramps, carpeting, cages, and even stereo systems, TVs, and VCRs. Until you step inside and check out what they have to offer, you can't imagine how efficiently and attractively they are designed.

Being mobile gives the groomer flexibility. From raising kids to showing dogs, the mobile groomer builds a work schedule custom-made to fit his or her needs. Prices range from around $20,000 for a trailer-type unit to $76,000 for the largest and most luxurious self-contained salons on wheels. Financing is available through the major auto manufacturers such as Ford and Chrysler or through a conventional bank loan. But be aware that the bank will want to see a detailed business plan.

When you consider the initial cost of starting a shop, the mobile looks even better. In a commercial location, you must pay first and last month's rent as well as leasehold improvements, which can easily total $10,000 to $15,000 once you get through with remodeling, electricity, and plumbing costs. Once your van is paid off—typically within five years at $800 to $900 a month—you will have an asset worth $25,000 or more if you have taken care of it properly.

While experienced shop groomers typically groom ten to twelve pets in a day, the mobile groomer usually grooms no more than six. However, when you consider the higher cost per job the mobile operator charges for such personalized service, you end up doing fewer pets and taking in the same amount of money. According to Dina Perry, president of Wag'n Tails Mobile Conversions of Elkhart, Indiana, the average mobile groomer makes at least $50,000 a year.

Of course, how much you make would depend upon how much you charge. Averaging six dogs per day at $65 per dog, and working five days per week, you could generate $8,580 per month or $102,960 annually. Subtracting your overhead, your gross profit would be $6,555 per month or $78,660 per year plus tips, according to information provided by Wag'n Tails. (To see how these numbers are crunched, check out www.wagntails.com/html/why/profit.htm.) Perry, who has also owned and operated grooming salons, a grooming school, a dryer company, and a boarding kennel, once had a fleet of twenty vans on the road. This innovative woman, who has been such a force in the mobile grooming industry, was named Groomer of the Century at the Cardinal Crystal Achievement Awards ceremony in 2000 at Intergroom—akin to a Lifetime Achievement Award at the Oscars.

When investigating the purchase of a mobile grooming van, you should educate yourself by checking out manufacturers' websites. For Perry's company, run by her son Dennis Gnetz, check www.wagntails.com. Odyssey Mobile Pet Grooming Vehicles of Wharton, New Jersey, building mobiles since 1979, can be found online at www.odysseyauto.com. Frank Weag, Odyssey's mobile van sales representative, runs the Mobile Van Roundup Rodeo at Groom Expo in Pennsylvania every September, a great place to check out makes and models. Ultimate Groomobiles of Sarasota, Florida, may be found online at www.ultimategroomobiles.com; Hanvey Specialty Engineering at www.groomingvans.com; and Amber's Mobile Pet Salons, Inc. at www.ambersmobilepetsalons.com. For a used mobile grooming van, the Petgroomer.com website features a comprehensive listing of used vans for sale. You usually only need a 10 to 20 percent downpayment on your mobile conversion van. If you have good credit, you can easily obtain financing. It is highly advisable to purchase your grooming van from a conversion company with previous experience in outfitting these units. Advertising is a snap; your customized van acts as a traveling billboard.

You've heard the pros, but what are the potential cons when it comes to mobile grooming? First, downtime for the mobile groomer's vehicle means no income. You'll want to check carefully the service and support options that are available.

"If the company truly cares for your business, they will send you replacement parts overnight and deal with vendors and repair shops themselves," says Terry E. Minix, president and CEO of J. T. Custom Works, another prominent conversion company (online at www.customvehicles.com). "Some conversion companies require you to have written authorization before repairs can take place. Most responsible manufactures have a policy that will allow the customer to choose where they would like to have repairs made to their vehicle."

Talk to other mobile groomers; most manufacturers will be glad to furnish references upon request.

Mobile grooming also has a self-contained ceiling as to the number of pets you can groom. In a mobile business, there is no room for expansion unless you purchase more vehicles. It can be done. You can make your business a family affair, with your spouse or adult children hitting the road in another van of their own. One of the most accomplished groomers in the industry, Melissa Verplank, started with a single mobile van and grew her business to six units. A national and international grooming champion and award-winning writer, Verplank has been a member and national coordinator of GroomTeam USA and is a prominent author in the grooming industry. She operates the Paragon School of Pet Grooming in Jenison, Michigan.

Tailor-made insurance policies are now provided for mobile operators by Gibson-Governor Agency, Inc. of Vienna, Ohio (www.gibsongovernor.com). Mobile groomers have their own organization, Professional Mobile Groomers International (PMGI).

If you are an independent spirit who desires the freedom of the open road while running your own grooming business, a career as a mobile groomer may be just the ticket for you.

Pet Grooming Potpourri

One of the best and worst things about grooming is that in this job, no two days are alike. You can cut down on stress and keep things running smoothly if you adhere to routine operational procedures from day one. You will soon develop your own policies regarding shop upkeep, scheduling, client relations, and safety and health issues. To keep your batteries charged and continue to learn and grow, it's also important to attend seminars and network with your fellow groomers. When you're working alone, isolation can become an occupational hazard.

Good Housekeeping and Antiseptic Procedures

One of the most important purchases you will make as a start-up grooming business is a good broom! The amount of hair that piles up each and every hour is astounding. If we could sell it by the bagful, we could all retire early. Just as in a beauty salon for humans, when a stylist is giving a haircut, there is bound to be hair on the floor. But in a beauty parlor, it gets swept up after each and every client. Can you imagine how you would feel if you had to wade through someone else's hair to get into the stylist's chair? It would be like having the hostess at an expensive restaurant show you to a table piled high with the previous patron's dirty dishes—not very appetizing!

It's the same story in the grooming salon. All too often busy groomers who are "on the clock" keep grooming dog after dog without sweeping or vacuuming the floor around their tables, totally oblivious to the fact that they are working knee-deep in hair. Can you think or a more unattractive sight for clients who pop their heads into the groom room to ooh and ahh at all those cute little critters?

The professional groomer should sweep up the hair and clean his or her table after each dog. End of story. If you can't get to it yourself and you have employees, use a little teamwork and help each other out. At least once a day, the place should be vacuumed thoroughly. Hair builds up in corners, on dryer filters, on top of and under the water heater, under the tubs, even migrating into the reception area. The stuff seems to have a mind of its own. It would be a shame to spend all this time and money planning and building your dream only to give the impression that you don't give a hoot about keeping it clean. Clients will appreciate the cleanliness of your shop, and they will want to keep coming back. After all, they are entrusting you with their precious pets, their surrogate children, and they need to feel that you are a responsible professional who provides a safe and sanitary environment for the animals in your care.

One of the nicest compliments a visitor can pay us is to remark on how fresh and clean the shop smells. Grooming can be a messy and smelly business. Dirty dog hair, "accidents" that occur on a daily basis with nervous pets, dogs that have just had a personal encounter with a skunk, wet towels, anal gland secretions, ear odors—you name it, bad smells come from myriad sources. Keeping them under control is a challenge.

Your grooming area must be cleaned and disinfected daily. If dog hair builds up in the crates or under the tub, it can provide a breeding ground for fleas, ticks, mange mites, bacteria, and mold. Sweeping and vacuuming often is an important first step, but the floor needs a good scrubbing with a deodorizing and disinfecting cleaner at least once a week. The product you choose should not only make the place look and smell clean, it should also eliminate viruses, bacteria, and fungi. Dander and sloughed off skin from pets can harbor all manner of infectious materials. Feces, urine, and other body fluids can spread parvovirus and many other diseases.

Your grooming table should be cleaned of hair and debris after each dog. Keep spray bottles of antiseptic cleaner handy to speed up this process and for immediate cleanup when accidents occur. Use a scrub brush to clean out the grooved surface of your grooming table. Cages and crates should be washed down at the end of each day. If they get soiled or hold pets with skin conditions, of course they will need cleaning immediately. Your job will be made easier if your cages have removable pans in the bottoms or your built-in cubbies have a washable surface such as Formica. The tub also needs a good scrubbing at the end of each workday.

Your clipper blades and scissors need frequent cleaning, too. An old toothbrush works well for removing hair and dirt from the blade teeth. If you have been clipping a dog with a skin condition, soak those blades in a disinfectant made for this purpose. Wipe your shears down with a germicidal cleaner, dry them thoroughly, then lubricate the hinges. The forceps you use to remove hair from dogs' ears are another potential source of contamination. Disinfect them after each and every use to avoid spreading ear infections among your furry clientele. If an animal has fleas or ticks, keep it separate from all other clients, get it into the tub for a flea or tick bath as soon as possible, and spray every area it has been in.

Beyond the cleaning and disinfecting of equipment, all groomers should learn basic clipper repair and maintenance. For students and veterans alike, hands-on workshops are held at every major grooming convention, covering clipper care, the causes and correction of common problems, the tools needed for routine repairs, and the use of blade coolants. We have invited a local sharpener to our shop to do a hands-on seminar on blade and shear care. Mastering these basic chores is not difficult and can save you a bundle.

By educating yourself on the safe use of pesticides in the shop, you can also be your own pest control expert. During flea season, use foggers to eliminate those pesky parasites in your shop at least once a week. When ticks are removed, drop them into a container of alcohol or dip to kill them. Never throw them in the trash bucket; they can escape and hatch out their young. Never handle ticks without gloves. They cause several diseases, including Lyme disease, Rocky Mountain spotted fever, tularemia, ehrlichiosis, and babesiosis. If you have groomed a pet with fleas or ticks, get those bags of contaminated hair out of the shop immediately. Having a client tell you that a dog picked up fleas at your shop is not the kind of word-of-mouth publicity you want to get around. (You should have discovered a flea infestation at the morning check-in, so this should never happen.)

A wide array of wonderful products is available to keep your workplace sanitary. Make sure the one you choose is effective against all viruses (including parvovirus), bacteria, and fungal spores. In a pinch, you can disinfect surfaces with a solution of one part chlorine bleach to thirty parts water, but if you splash this stuff on your clothing, you'll be wearing polka dots! Electric air purifiers work wonders keeping the air fresh and clean. We use the same air purification system that has been used to clean up natural disasters, and you notice the difference immediately after hitting the "on" switch. (www.austinair.com)

Last but not least, wash your hands, preferably with an antibacterial hand cleaner. This will protect your own health as well as that of the pets in your care. Just like bad news travels fast, so does a good reputation. If your shop is clean and sanitary, the word will get around, and you will receive recommendations from happy clients, veterinarians, and fellow pet grooming professionals.

Pet Health Issues

For groomers, it is vitally important to check the condition of every single pet that comes through your door when it is being dropped off for grooming. Ask the owner if there have been any changes in the pet's health since its last appointment. For new clients, ask if you need to be aware of any existing ailments or conditions. If a pet is under the care of a veterinarian, you need to know if it will be at risk during the grooming process. If you have any doubts or misgivings, by all means contact the vet to get the proper clearance before you groom the animal, or have the owner rebook and return with a letter from the vet to protect yourself.

There are many instances when it would be advisable to have the owner sign a release form to protect you in case the pet has an adverse reaction to the grooming procedure. "Red flags" include a coat so severely matted that clipping and/or brushing could cause skin irritation; dogs with heart conditions, seizure disorders, cancer, or joint problems; or dogs that are frail or elderly. You may not be aware that a dog has a disk problem in its back or a trick knee until it cries out in pain as it is being groomed or bathed. Take the time to ask the right questions and have the release forms signed and kept on file.

Observe the dog's skin condition as you go over it with the owner. If there are open sores, scabs, and obvious infections, you should not attempt to groom the pet; refer it to a veterinarian instead. This is not only for your own protection, but to avoid exposure to other dogs in your care.

You should also require that all the dogs you take in to your establishment be up-to-date on their shots. Rabies, caused by a virus that attacks the nervous system, is increasingly widespread. Although it is far more prevalent in wild animals than in the pet population, dogs and cats can get it, too. After entering the body, the virus multiplies, causing encephalitis (inflammation of the brain). Untreated, this disease is always fatal to pets and people. To protect yourself and your staff, gather vaccination information when you take dogs in and make sure you update your files.

FUR MAGNOLIAS GROOMING

402 Maple Lane, Plainfield, MA 02011
Telephone (508) 555–8770

Dematting

February 1, 2011

Dear Mary Brown,

Your pet's health and proper care are first and foremost in our minds and in our hearts here at Fur Magnolias Grooming. Due to the matting and tangling of Max's coat today, it will require extra work to complete his grooming. Dematting is not included as part of the base price, and there will be an extra charge today. The rate for dematting is $35 per hour in addition to your pet's base price for grooming.

Please understand that the process of dematting can be uncomfortable for your pet and may sometimes cause skin irritations. We will provide your pet with a medicated bath if it will increase his comfort. There is an additional charge for medicated baths.

If the dematting process is too uncomfortable or strenuous for Max, we will be in touch with you to discuss the alternatives. Please leave us a telephone number where you can be reached.

If you agree to this contract, please sign below.

I, the undersigned, grant permission to Fur Magnolias Grooming to demat my pet. I understand that there may be complications, and I will not hold Fur Magnolias Grooming responsible.

_____   _____

Signature   Date

_____

Phone

FUR MAGNOLIAS GROOMING

402 Maple Lane, Plainfield, MA 02011
Telephone (508) 555–8770

Stripping the Coat

February 1, 2011

Dear Mary Brown,

Your pet's health and proper care are first and foremost in our minds and in our hearts here at Fur Magnolias Grooming. Due to Max's condition of severe tangling and matting, we will need to shave him today. Please understand that it is our belief that this is the kindest and most humane thing to do for Max. The matting is too severe, and the dematting process itself would be painful and leave the coat severely damaged.

We will perform this procedure with the utmost care; however, there is a possibility of skin irritation and nicking. If we feel a medicated bath will soothe the irritated skin, we will provide that service for your pet at an additional charge.

If you understand this contract, please sign below.

I, the undersigned, grant permission to Fur Magnolias Grooming to perform the necessary grooming procedure to remove the matting from my pet. I understand that there may be complications, and I will not hold Fur Magnolias Grooming responsible for these complications.

_____   _____
Signature   Date

_____
Phone

Some clients perceive this information-gathering as a bother, but don't be put off. Proof of rabies vaccination is required by most states in order to get a dog licensed. Most pet owners will appreciate your diligence and professionalism. Even though rabies is a far greater threat to humans in developing countries, every year an estimated 40,000 people in the United States must receive postexposure prophylaxis (PEP) treatment, a twenty-eight-day series of shots, following exposure to this dreaded disease.

Be sure to check with your local health department on the laws regarding dog bites. In Massachusetts, a dog bite must be reported to the local health authorities and to the animal control officer in your community. Whether the dog is up-to-date on its shots or not, if it has bitten someone it must be quarantined at home for a ten-day period, after which it will be examined by the animal control officer to make sure that it is healthy before it is released from quarantine.

Pet animals become exposed to rabies when they tangle with wild animals, usually through a bite wound. When you are handling dogs that have been sprayed by a skunk or outdoor cats that hunt, you are putting yourself at risk if these pets do not have current rabies vaccinations. Rabies can be transmitted through bodily fluids, so if a pet's coat has blood or saliva from an infected animal, you could contract the disease through a cut or scratch on your own skin.

You must also exercise care when dealing with puppies. They usually start to receive their vaccinations at six to eight weeks of age, followed by three or four booster shots at two- to four-week intervals. These youngsters should not be exposed to other dogs until they have completed their second series of shots. Healthy adult dogs that are up-to-date on their shots are protected from infectious diseases such as parvovirus, but in the case of an unvaccinated pup, such an illness could be fatal.

The three basic vaccinations all dogs should receive include a multipurpose one known as DHPP, which guards against distemper, hepatitis, parainfluenza, and parvovirus (if it also includes leptospirosis antigen, it is called DHLPP); Bordetella, the most common cause of so-called kennel cough; and the rabies vaccine. A rabies shot is good for either one year or three. Whether given annually or every three years, it's the same vaccine. Boosting it annually produces a stronger immunity for the pet. Most states require rabies shots for dogs and cats. Most states now require dogs to be vaccinated annually. Ultimately, it is the owner's responsibility to keep dogs properly vaccinated, but to be on the safe side and to protect your clients and staff, make this record keeping part of your regular intake procedure. Most grooming software has the fields to record this information and will automatically notify you if a pet is overdue.

Having a good relationship with the vets in your area is also vitally important. When you become known as a conscientious and caring professional, vets will send their clients your way for grooming. You will also need to keep the lines of communication open. A client might tell you, "The vet said my dog was clipper-burned at your shop," or "The vet told me my dog picked up kennel cough the last time you groomed him." A personal and professional relationship with the vet will help you to discuss the situation in a professional manner. Unfortunately, some vets blame the groomer for everything from impacted anal glands to the common cold, but many times, clients' reports of what the vet said get severely distorted in translation. A mutually respectful relationship with the vet is your best insurance against unwarranted accusations. "Clipper burn" is probably the most common complaint that groomers hear about. It is the result of damaging the skin during the grooming process either due to blade friction or a hot clipper blade. Keep in mind that even running a #10 blade against a dog's skin can cause damage to the tissue. The good news is that it doesn't have to happen. Use gentleness and care when clipping. Make sure your blades are not overheated when you groom. Feel them with your fingers and change them often. Spray them with a cooling agent as you work. When clipping white or light-colored dogs like bichons, poodles, Maltese, or West Highland terriers, don't use a blade that cuts very close on sensitive areas. Instead of a #30, a #15, or a #10 blade, use a #9 or a #7F. Also make sure you are not grooming with dull blades, another potential cause of this condition.

Sometimes the groomer gets blamed for clipper burn if the animal's sensitive skin causes a reaction to the grooming. Other times, dogs whose coats have been badly neglected end up irritated and itchy after a clipdown. These pets may go home and start digging and scratching themselves to the point of self-mutilation, and the irate owner will call to accuse you of "cutting" the dog. Your best bet is to explain that some dogs, like some people, have highly sensitive skin and get a rash from shaving. If the animal was in rough shape before you even started, explain the need for more frequent groomings and resolve to examine all pets more carefully in the future. This is another instance when a waiver is essential. Offer a free medicated bath to soothe the pet—and the owner, too.

A good working relationship with a vet is a blessing if an injury to a pet occurs in your shop. It is unfortunate and extremely upsetting, but occasionally accidents do happen. A nicked ear, a cut footpad, an eye irritation from shampoo, or a scissor cut—these situations require a vet's prompt attention.

The first rule to follow when an injury occurs is to tell the pet's owner. It's scary, but you have to do it. Nine times out of ten, it's a minor matter—skin irritated from brushing, a scratch, or a nick—but as an honest professional, you must document the incident and let the owner know about it immediately. Offer a product to help heal it, at no charge, of course. Offer the next grooming "on the house." If you feel it is your fault, you should volunteer to cover any veterinary expenses. Your liability insurance should cover such medical care. Most people understand that a dog can wiggle or jump unexpectedly as you are working on it. They are living creatures, after all, not stuffed animals. Being honest and up-front in such situations is important for your own integrity and peace of mind as well. Follow up the visit by calling to see how the pet is doing.

No matter how upsetting a situation is, we can always learn from it. Grooming, performed with sharp instruments such as shears, clipper blades, and dematting tools, requires total concentration. By paying attention and adhering to safe practices in the workplace, we can take steps to keep such instances from occurring.

Of course, there are times when you will detect an injury or a medical condition that has nothing to do with you. We see these pets more frequently than their vets, and because we examine and handle them from head to tail, we often notice things the owner might miss when giving Fido a pat or a tickle once or twice a day. It is important to tell the owner of anything out of the ordinary you discover while grooming a pet. It is also important to document it. Occasionally, we all run into that problem customer who wants to blame everything on us. It's a worst-case scenario, but if such a matter ends up in court, you will need proper documentation to prove you are not at fault.

The most common causes for concern that groomers discover when caring for pets are tumors and growths. They are not hard to spot on short-coated dogs, but they can be easily missed under a thick or long coat. Older dogs are prone to warts, making the job of grooming without nicking them very tricky. Most fatty tumors you detect are probably not malignant, but those solidly adhering to bone may indicate cancer is present. Dogs get all the same cancers as people, including mammary tumors. Dogs that wince or cry when you touch their muzzle may have oral tumors or dental problems. If you see tartar buildup on the teeth or notice that the pet's breath has a foul odor, you need to convey this information to the owner.

You may notice that a dog is limping or doesn't want one of its paws touched. You may see a discharge from the ears, eyes, or genital area. The skin may have lesions or evidence of parasites like fleas, ticks, lice, or mange mites. You may uncover an abscess or wound the owner does not know about. A normally happy pet may appear listless or overly agitated on a particular visit. A dog may have a seizure in your shop. All of these conditions need to be brought to the owner's attention immediately. In cases of serious illness, the sooner the pet gets medical treatment, the better its chances for a full recovery. It is so gratifying to have an owner thank you for noticing something he or she could have missed. It's fun to be a hero!

You must be careful informing the client about anything out of the ordinary you encounter while grooming. First, do not diagnose; that's a vet's job. Even if you suspect something as common as ear mites in a cat, remember that those tiny organisms can only be seen under a microscope. Do not suggest treatment; merely tell the owner calmly and without drama that you think Fluffy needs to see the vet to have the situation checked.

Tact is essential. Owners may have financial problems and feel they are unable to afford treatment. They may be in denial or emotionally unable to cope with a pet's illness. They may react defensively, blaming the messenger, which in this case happens to be you. In any event, as a caring professional, you must tell them what you have observed and recommend they seek the proper medical help.

Early Arrivals and Late Pickups

One of the most common complaints for all groomers, especially those who work out of their homes, is the customer who arrives early and picks up late. Having your grooming business where you live can be a blessing and a curse. Stories abound of impatient clients parked in the driveway with the motor running as you sip your morning coffee or emerge from the shower. Just because you work where you live, some folks think it's perfectly acceptable to drop off or pick up their pets any time they please.

Educating your clientele on your hours of operation is up to you. You should post a sign listing the hours your business is open. When animals are dropped off in the morning, be sure to say, "Last pickup is by six o'clock," or whatever time you deem appropriate. People need to realize that groomers have a life, too. We have dinner engagements, kids' baseball games, evening courses to attend, and social functions, just like everybody else.

If owners pick up late more than once, it's up to you to tactfully tell them that you can no longer groom their pets unless they can pick up on time. Some groomers institute a "late fee," and in our shop it's posted as one dollar per minute for pets left after hours. Whether we institute the charge or not, no money can give us back the time we miss with our families. We also have a "three strikes" rule, but after the first offense, we seem to get our point across.

If John Q. Public pulls into your driveway while you're still in your pajamas, have the self-control not to go to the door until you are ready to open. People do not do that to their doctor, dentist, or hairstylist; why is it okay to do it to their groomer? When you do open your doors, again explain your hours of operation. Some folks need to hear it more than once.

We open at 7:30 a.m. five days a week to accommodate commuters and teachers, and they appreciate it. But we still occasionally encounter the impatient patron banging on the door at 7:15, irate because we are not open yet. It is important to remain calm and professional. This is the customer's problem, not yours. You can be sure if you do open at 7:15 this time, the next time this guy will arrive at 7!

We make reminder calls to each client a day or two before the appointment, always stating our shop's drop-off times. We require the dogs to be in by 9:30 a.m. so each groomer will have his or her workload for the day and can get the "roughing" work out of the way before the dogs are bathed. If a person arrives an hour late without phoning to let us know, it can disrupt a groomer's schedule and cause a lot of stress.

We have a sign posted that reads:

Dogs arriving after 9:30 may need to be rescheduled. We take call-ins and clients from our waiting list after 9:30 to ensure a full workday for our pet grooming professionals. We appreciate your understanding.

This gives us a little leeway to either take in the late arrival or reschedule the appointment for another day.

Of course, at times there are extenuating circumstances. We are happy to make an exception, but in such cases the client has usually called ahead to make special arrangements. We also enter the arrival time along with the date on the computer worksheet when we rebook the pet. Walking that fine line between enjoying the customers' friendship and commanding their respect can be a challenge. You need to set your boundaries and stick to them.

Groomer Health Issues

Grooming takes a toll on the body. It is a labor-intensive job. First of all, most groomers stand all day, straining the legs and contributing to varicose veins. Performing some grooming functions while seated on a stool will give your legs a rest. Use a cushioned mat under your table and move around as you work to lessen the strain and prevent blood from pooling in your legs. All groomers need to wear comfortable shoes that offer support. Footwear designed for nursing seems to fit the bill. Open-toed shoes are never appropriate, as you could drop sharp tools on your toes or step on something highly unappetizing as you go about your work.

Today's groomers have the benefits of hydraulic and electric tables and ramps or folding stairs to help get big dogs in and out of the tub, but there is still a large amount of lifting you need to do in this profession. It's crucial to the health of your back that you learn to lift correctly, using your legs to do most of the work and asking for help when you need it. You are not Superman or Wonder Woman!

Scissoring is an activity that uses repetitive motion of the hands and wrists, a prime cause of tendinitis and carpal tunnel syndrome. The continual overuse of the fine muscles of the hands and wrists places a strain on a large nerve that extends from the wrist to the fingertips. Carpal tunnel syndrome is painful and debilitating; it can end a grooming career. It results in numbness of the thumb and fingers and a loss of muscle control as well as chronic pain. Working with the proper tools—scissors that are the right size and weight for your hands, clippers that are not too bulky and heavy—goes a long way toward preventing this occupational hazard. Even learning to brush in long, slow strokes using the weight of your body as opposed to short, jerky motions will save your hands and back. Many groomers wear wrist supports to prevent or relieve this condition. It is treatable through surgery, but that requires several weeks of incapacitation and recuperation, and it is not always 100 percent successful.

Our workplaces can be like obstacle courses. Electrical cords attached to dryers and clippers are easy to trip over. Making sure we never touch electrical equipment with wet hands may seem like a no-brainer, but in the hectic rush of a busy day, one can easily become distracted and forget this fundamental safety rule.

Stress is another common health hazard to groomers. We work by the clock, and time is money. We strive to please a wide spectrum of the general public. Our work can be unpredictable and sometimes dangerous. We are not always treated with respect. To preserve your sanity, it is necessary that you learn to handle stress. Groomer burnout is a recognized phenomenon in this business.

We need to take good care of number one. Good eating and sleeping habits go a long way toward preparing us for all the situations we face in a day of working with animals that can be uncooperative and owners who can be quite demanding. Groomers are notorious for their poor eating habits. It is important to feed your body properly in any occupation, but when you are on the clock, bringing healthy snacks to graze on is great for the groom room. Sugar and caffeine will feel good in the moment, but then comes the crash. You should make the time to eat a nourishing breakfast, and sit down away from the dog hair for a well-deserved lunch break.

As physically challenging as grooming can be, it is not exercise. Aerobic activity such as walking, running, biking, or taking some classes at the gym protects our cardiovascular health, builds our endurance, and helps us deal with stress. Weight training improves our overall conditioning and strengthens our bones as it improves our metabolism. Going outside during the day for a breath of fresh air or a walk around the block provides a mental and physical respite from the harried routine.

Taking care of your physical needs is key, but to succeed in this field it is equally important to develop a healthy mental attitude. You need to learn to take things in stride and not sweat the small stuff. It's easier said than done, but once in a while, it helps to get a reality check. We are dealing with pet grooming, not brain surgery! We do our best to treat the animals with loving kindness, to improve our grooming knowledge and skill, and to style these pets to please their owners. We soon learn, however, that we can't please everybody. Some people have demands that we cannot fulfill. Sometimes things happen that are beyond our control. Anger over problems that we can't immediately solve, the hectic pace of our working environment, financial pressures, family issues, unreasonable clients—all of these things can overwhelm us, robbing us of our energy and our joy.

Keeping our problems bottled up inside does not make them go away. Having a trusted partner, friend, or family member to turn to can be a huge help. We may need to talk to a therapist or counselor to get to the root of our problems and start feeling better. One thing is certain: If you don't deal with your stress, it will manifest itself in physical symptoms like sleep disturbances, depression, anxiety, fatigue, or serious illness.

Taking the time to pamper yourself also helps maintain your mental equilibrium. Yoga, meditation, writing in your journal, reading, planting a flower bed, learning how to say no—there are many ways to counteract the stresses of everyday life.

Laughter is a great stress reliever. No matter how overwhelming a situation feels, chances are you can find a humorous way of looking at it.

Groomers like to joke with each other, saying that we are "no-lifers." There is some truth to that. We sometimes focus on our jobs to the detriment of family life and friendships. We all need to achieve that balance between doing a job we love and nourishing ourselves with supportive relationships and fun activities that recharge our batteries and feed our souls.

Transmittable Diseases

Pet grooming professionals also need to be aware of zoonotic diseases, those illnesses that are transmittable from animals to humans. We have already mentioned tick-borne diseases. The most important thing to remember is to wear gloves and use tweezers when pulling ticks off pets. Ticks spread their diseases to humans not only by attaching themselves to our skin but also through our contact with their bacteria-laden fluids.

Such internal parasites as hookworm, roundworm, heartworm, trichinosis, ringworm, and tapeworm can be passed to people who come in contact with animal feces. When you're working with animals, never pick up food without scrubbing your hands first.

Ringworm, a fungal infection, is more prevalent in cats than in dogs. You can pick it up through spores in the air as well as by contact with an infected animal. When you scratch the resulting ring-shaped lesions, the disease spreads as new spores are released. It is highly contagious to people you come in contact with and can eventually lead to kidney damage.

Learn to look for its symptoms. Pets with crusty sores behind their ears, small round scabby or bald patches on their bodies, and/or sparse hair growth around their eyes may have ringworm or mange. I prefer to let the vet handle pets with this problem. If animals infected with ringworm have been in your shop, treat every area they have come in contact with, using a germicidal disinfectant or a bleach solution. These spores can linger in cages and on tables for as long as fourteen days.

Animal bites are the source of a variety of illnesses. Rabies, septicemia, and streptococcal and staphylococcal infections are all bacterial infections transmittable primarily through bite wounds. When working with animals, it is vital to maintain up-to-date tetanus shots. If you get bitten, bleeding should not be stopped immediately because your system rids itself of bacteria this way. Thoroughly wash the wound with an antibacterial soap, then assess whether you need to go to the hospital for stitches.

Canine brucellosis, another transmittable illness, causes symptoms similar to those of mononucleosis: fever, chills, headaches, joint pain, and fatigue. When seeking medical treatment for symptoms like these, be sure to tell your doctor that you work with pets.

Coccidia and giardia are microorganisms present in the intestines of cats and dogs. When pets get stressed, as they often do in grooming or boarding situations, they become symptomatic, resulting in vomiting, diarrhea, and eventually coat and skin damage. Keeping your shop cleaned and disinfected will protect you from catching these diseases.

Chlamydia is transmitted by cats that show symptoms through runny eyes, sometimes with the "third eyelid" elevated in the corner of the eye. Cats can and should be vaccinated against this illness. In humans it looks like conjunctivitis, but it can cause pneumonia and genital infections, transmittable by sexual contact.

Because of the danger of toxoplasmosis, no pregnant groomer should work on cats or clean their cages or litter boxes. Cats contract this disease from raw meat or garden vegetables. It is highly transmittable when humans come in contact with cat feces. It causes miscarriages and birth defects in mammals, including humans. Because it may be asymptomatic, the best way to protect groomers who are pregnant is to have them avoid cleaning litter boxes and cat cages at home and at work.

A somewhat rarer ailment known as cat scratch fever is another malady spread by contact with infected cats. Mimicking a case of the flu, it causes a general feeling of malaise as well as fever, swollen glands and lymph nodes, and pustules. It is carried in the animal's saliva or bacteria on its claws and is transmittable through a scratch, bite, or lick from an infected cat. Left untreated, it can cause brain and liver disorders in humans. It can be diagnosed with a skin test.

Tularemia is a bacterial infection transmitted to humans through bites and scratches or bodily discharges of infected dogs or cats. Pets get it from fleas or ticks; outdoor pets can also pick it up from infected rodents when they hunt. It manifests itself in humans as sores on the hands, swollen lymph nodes, muscular pain, diarrhea, vomiting, and pneumonia.

Rabies is the most deadly of all the zoonotic diseases. It is diagnosed by euthanizing the suspected animal and having its brain tested. If you have been bitten by an unvaccinated pet that shows its symptoms, you need to begin an immediate regimen of twenty-eight daily injections, administered in the stomach or back. To protect yourself and your employees, all animals in your care should be required to have up-to-date rabies vaccinations—no excuses and no exceptions.

Chemical Contamination

To rid pets of fleas and ticks, groomers use pesticides. These highly effective products are a boon to pets and their owners, but their frequent use can be harmful to your health. Chemicals that spell doom to fleas and ticks can be absorbed through your skin, causing a host of debilitating problems over time. Some groomers have become disabled with severe and irreversible nerve damage caused by the improper use of pesticides.

It is important to familiarize yourself with flea and tick products. The safest ones use natural substances such as pyrethrins, citrus peel, and other botanicals. Although these substances knock down fleas and ticks fast, they offer very little residual effect. It takes the more potent organophosphates to do that. These contain cholinesterase inhibitors, causing nerve damage to the parasite by suppressing its immune system. Unfortunately, they do the same to unprotected humans.

With the highly effective shampoos available on the market, as well as products like Capstar and monthly topicals, the days of dipping pets are rare. If you do need to use dip, make sure your bathing area is ventilated by an exhaust fan, preferably installed over the tub. Read the labels on all pesticides. Do not mix and match products, which can cause chemical overload to the pets you are treating. Dilute strictly according to directions, and make sure you label everything! Be sure to ask clients what flea and tick control products they are currently using before you treat an animal.

The signs of chemical overload are the same in humans as they are in pets: muscle weakness, headaches, dizziness, salivation, thirst, frequent urination, fatigue, diarrhea, and nausea leading to coma, convulsions, and death. If you notice any of these symptoms in a pet, rinse them thoroughly and get veterinary care immediately

Honing Your Skills

It's important to keep up-to-date on all phases of your profession. Grooming styles and breed standards change, equipment keeps improving, and new techniques are constantly being introduced. In addition, there is no substitute for the camaraderie you experience when you gather with your peers.

In-Service Training

Truly successful people in every field know that there is always room for improvement. The best way to continue your education as a groomer is through involvement in a grooming association and attendance at workshops and seminars. Working on your own as a groomer, especially when you are based at home, can sometimes be an isolating experience. When you join a groomers' association you will meet new friends and colleagues and keep up-to-date on what's happening in your industry. These associations have sprung up in every state and many foreign countries as well. Do not feel like a poor relation because you are a new kid on the block or a home groomer. Many of the industry's top groomers, speakers, and judges came from the ranks of home groomers just like you!

Become active in your association. As is the case with most professional organizations, there is always a dedicated core of volunteers who do the lion's share of the work on behalf of everybody else but we cannot underestimate the benefits of the camaraderie, networking and self- improvement that you will receive from participating. Our own New England Pet Grooming Professionals (www.nepgp .com), founded thirty-one years ago, holds its annual show in July, drawing attendees and competitors from all over the country and boasts members from several states outside the New England region.

There are also national organizations for professional pet groomers that offer benefits; hold conventions, competitions, and seminars; and offer professional certification. The largest one is the National Dog Groomers Association of America (NDGAA), with approximately 3,000 members. Established in 1969, it offers such benefits as health, disability, liability, and life insurance as well as retirement plans. Check it out at www.nationaldoggroomers.com.

Certification

When groomers get together, the question of whether to become certified always provokes a lively debate. Because we are not required to have formal licensing like professional stylists for people do, virtually anybody can advertise himself or herself as a professional pet groomer. Achieving professional certification is one way you can communicate to your clientele that you are a trained member of your profession who has passed certain tests to achieve formal recognition of your knowledge and skill.

Certification involves both written and hands-on testing of the correct way to groom the various breeds according to the official breed standard. The written test covers dog and cat health, anatomy, and breed information. Once you have become certified, you can and should advertise it at your place of business, in your yellow pages and newspaper ads, and on your business cards. You will gain the title of Certified Master Groomer or Master Stylist.

In addition to the NDGAA, there are other professional organizations that offer certification. Look into all the different programs before you decide. Becoming certified takes time, money, and effort on your part. You will need to travel to the sites where testing takes place and provide your own dogs for the practical parts of the test. Becoming certified is by no means a requirement to becoming successful in this profession. It does, however, carry with it a certain pride in the accomplishment of having completed the process. It boosts your confidence and self-esteem. In addition, if the day ever comes to pass when the grooming profession requires vocational licensing, being certified may give you a leg up on your fellow professionals who have not achieved this title.

Many groomers shy away from the licensing issue because they envision a dreaded tangle of bureaucratic red tape and governmental fees. Others have tunnel vision, wishing to avoid the issue entirely as they toil away in their own little cocoons. On the other side, many feel that vocational licensing may be a much needed step forward for our profession, arguing that it would bring more respect

Certification Listings and Titles

National Certified Master Groomer (NCMG) offered by NDGAA
(724-962-2711 or www.nauticom.net/www/ndga)

Companion Animal Hygienist (CAH) offered by World Wide Pet Supplies Association
(WWWPSA) (818-447-2222 or www.wwpsa.com)

Certified Master Groomer (CMG) offered by International
Professional Groomers (800-258-4765)

ISCC Certified offered by the International Society of Canine Cosmetologists
(972-414-9715 or www.petstylist.com)

from the public and make it easier to command the prices that we deserve. Others feel that for the protection of consumers—in this case, pet owners—licensing would ensure that those to whom they entrust their precious pets have met minimum standards for proper care and safety. The debate continues. Because it could affect us so directly, this is one area in which professional groomers need to keep themselves informed.

Grooming Shows and Competitions

Nationally and internationally, grooming conventions seem to get bigger and more numerous every year. These events combine grooming competitions, educational seminars, trade shows, and hands-on grooming demonstrations under one roof. Some groomers save their tips all year long to finance their attendance at such events.

The trade show exposes groomers to the latest in grooming equipment, from shears to shampoos. Shop owners can upgrade their salons with state-of-the-art equipment offered at special show prices. The largest of these events are Intergroom in New Jersey, Groom Expo in Pennsylvania and California, Jerry Schinberg's All American Grooming Competition in Illinois (the oldest of these events, begun in 1973), Atlanta Pet Fair in Georgia, Super Zoo in Las Vegas, NDGAA shows in Florida and South Carolina, US Pet Pro Classic in Texas, and Southern California Groomers Association Show in California.

As a neophyte groomer, the first time you find yourself ringside at a grooming competition will be an unforgettable experience. There you will witness the talented fingers of skilled groomers performing their magic, transforming overgrown furballs into exquisitely sculpted examples of the breed hiding under all that hair. Poodles, terriers, sporting breeds, even mixed breeds—grooming contestants compete in several divisions for cash prizes, trophies, ribbons, and medals.

Intergroom, the gala international convention held in New Jersey each April, celebrated its thirtieth anniversary in 2010. Begun by Shirlee and Larry Kalstone, this prestigious show is now owned and organized by Christine DeFilippo, who estimated its total cash awards for 2010 were in the vicinity of $40,000. Its International Groomer of the Year competition features the top groomers from all over the world. Groomers compete in six different classes: (1) Poodles, (2) Terriers, (3) Handstripping (dogs whose hair is plucked or stripped out rather than clippered), (4) Spaniels and Other Sporting Dogs, (5) All Other Purebreds, and (6) Mixed Breed/Miscellaneous (dogs of mixed-breed parentage plus any pedigreed dogs trimmed in styles other than the recognized breed standard). To compete in this event, a groomer must have previously been awarded a First Place at a recognized regional contest. This competition is considered by many to be the Olympic competition of the grooming world. For the groomer that's just getting started in the industry, DeFilippo said, "At Intergroom, a novice groomer would get, at the very least, a totally eye-opening experience." The level of grooming is exceptional.

In 2000 DeFilippo instituted the Rising Star Competition, an event open to novice and intermediate groomers. Cash prizes and ribbons as well as gift certificates and free attendance at industry educational events make this highly attractive to newcomers to the contest world.

GroomExpo, held each September in Hershey, Pennsylvania, bills itself as the world's biggest educational seminar and trade show for pet grooming professionals. In 2009 it drew 4,500 attendees and featured 170 exhibitors' booths. It also features grooming competitions awarding more than $30,000 in prizes, according to show owner Sally Liddick. In its Creative Styling contest, groomers let their imaginations run wild with color, costume, and whimsy, dressing themselves up as part of their chosen theme. No longer limited to the grooming industry, this show, held by Barkleigh Productions, attracts professionals from the boarding, pet sitting, and training arenas as well.

To find out about such national and regional events, you can check the listings at www.petgroomer.com or at the Pet Groomers' Lounge (www.groomers.com). Trade magazines such as *Groomer to Groomer, Grooming Business Magazine,* and *Pet Age* also feature calendar listings of these events.

The Contest Bug

Once you have attended a few grooming competitions, you may start thinking about competing yourself. Watch out: You've just been bitten by the contest bug! It takes time and effort to compete. There's a lot more to it than a few hours spent under the bright lights of the contest ring.

First of all, you need the right dog. Unlike AKC shows, which judge dogs on their conformation (how closely they conform to the breed standard), grooming competitions are judged according to how well the dog is groomed according to the breed profile. What's the difference? The breed profile is the correct visual appearance of that particular breed, based on the accepted grooming patterns established by each individual breed club. You still need a good example of the breed to begin with. A poodle or bichon needs a fluffy coat for scissoring; a cocker spaniel needs a full coat that falls well over its body contours. In other words, the dog needs good conformation with a good haircut on top of it.

Next, you need to grow that coat out to the correct length, usually eight weeks of growth, according to the contest rules. Make sure that you read the rules carefully before you fill out the entry form. If you have any questions, call the show organizer. Plan to get to the contest site in plenty of time; newcomers tend to get butterflies, and you will be calmer if you are not rushed.

Besides being beautiful, your contest dog must be well behaved. No matter how handsome he is, if he nips the judge, you'll be disqualified. You need to be able to finish grooming in the allotted time, usually one to two hours. Your dog must be bathed and fluffed before you enter the ring, either that morning or the day before. In the prejudging phase, the judge will examine the animal from head to tail to make sure it has sufficient coat growth and is clean, brushed out, and free from tangles, parasites, and skin diseases.

You should look your best when you enter the ring. Contestants should leave the jeans at home, choosing to look every bit as well groomed as their dogs. You also need to have the right mental attitude. It can be nerve-racking to groom in front of an audience for the first time, aware of the clock ticking away precious minutes. You need a competitive spirit and a cool head. Even if you do not place, you will learn from the experience. Most judges are more than willing to evaluate your work when the contest is over, helping you to do better the next time out. If you've been bitten by the bug, you'll probably be back to compete again!

GroomTeam USA

In 1987, a new program brought together the country's most successful groomers to represent the United States in international grooming competition. Thus was born GroomTeam USA. Groomers compete for their place on this team by piling up the points at sanctioned contests nationwide. The GroomTeam committee keeps track of contest results, tabulating point totals, and the six groomers with the most points win a place on the USA squad. Corporate contributions and its own fund-raising efforts finance the team, covering everything from travel expenses to snazzy red, white, and blue uniforms. The USA team has brought home the gold on may occasions, intensifying the competitive spirit among the best of the best. Some of its illustrious members, such as Diane Betelak of New York and Marea Tully and Carrie Prest of Massachusetts, have sprung from the ranks of home groomers. There is nothing wrong with dreaming—if the idea of representing your country in international competition appeals to you, then while you're at it, dream big!

12 Marketing and Public Relations

You already know you love working with pets, but can you make a living at it? Will your income maintain and eventually improve your standard of living? Will it finance your retirement? Before you take this life-changing plunge, you will need to test the waters by familiarizing yourself with the economic climate of your community. You will also need to become your own personal Madison Avenue when it comes to announcing your arrival on the scene.

Setting Your Prices

Before you set the prices on your services, you will need to do some market research in your community. Establishing what your service commands in dollars and cents will depend on where you live. The cost of living varies widely in different areas of the country, and prices for pet grooming services fluctuates accordingly. Hold on to this research information. It may be valuable data for future reference.

Although the government does not allow standardized prices within any industry, when groomers gather at seminars and trade shows, one of the most frequent questions they ask each other is, "How much do you charge for [fill in the breed]?" Comparing notes on prices is often the number one topic when they start chatting. Surprisingly, we never hear them talk about how they arrive at their prices.

In any business, the bottom line in figuring pricing is always based on your cost of operation combined with sufficient compensation to make a profit. To succeed in business, you need to know how to figure out the average cost of your services. Your profit margin depends on how much you spend as well as how much you take in.

Interestingly, a survey by one of our industry magazines found that pet grooming professionals with the highest profit margins did not necessarily charge the highest prices. They simply managed their businesses more efficiently, holding down their overhead costs for supplies, labor, and advertising. Some groomers who sold pet food took a lower markup on the food but used a higher markup on dry goods and boutique items. They used the food as a "leader" and a convenience for their customers, but they were pricier on impulse items and luxury goods than the big chains. Top performers know their market and fine-tune their prices accordingly. It helps to define your business to both yourself and the community as a "specialty service." You may not be able to compete with the big pet industry chain stores, but you don't have to. You are marketing something quite different, its value based upon the highly personal connection you offer your clients. These chain stores can spend millions trying to discover why independent pet groomers continue to succeed and lead the market, and the answer is: *you!* You are your own secret weapon.

Groomers usually have a base price for each breed. We have a ball park on breeds and base prices as well, but never give a quote without seeing a pet first. A pet owner's version of "matted" and a professional groomer's version can be worlds apart when they've been using a pin brush to keep their malamute in shape! According to a 2009 Petgroomer.com survey, the average fees for the top six breeds were as follows: miniature poodles (in a basic "lamb" or "kennel" trim), $40; miniature poodles in fancy patterns, $45; cocker spaniels, $45; shih tzus, $38; bichon frises, $42; golden retrievers, $55; and miniature schnauzers, $39. Prices tend to be higher on the East and West Coasts. These figures are averages, taken from more than 3,400 participants. Extras are usually tacked on to the base price. Most groomers will allow fifteen minutes or so for dematting or extra brushing of a dog's coat, but after that, an additional hourly dematting rate (varying widely from $10 to $60 per hour) kicks in. Flea baths and dips, medicated baths, expelling anal glands, deskunking and deodorizing treatments, hot oil treatments, tooth brushing, nail grinding, and extra time allotted for a "tough strip" (shaving down a severely matted coat) are typical add-on items. Some attach a "handling charge" for dogs that have behavior problems. We have a menu of services above our reception area so our customers can request additional care at drop-off.

Because time is money, your speed in grooming also plays a role (this will improve as you become more experienced). There are industry workshops offered by

Dogs

Poodles		Collie (rough)	$65
Toy	$40	Old English Sheepdog	$65
Mini	$40	Afghan Hound	$75
Standard	$75	Golden Retriever	$50
Terriers		Labrador Retriever	$45
Schnauzers		Dachshund	
Mini	$40	Smooth	$25
Standard	$50	Wirehair	$40
Giant	$65	Longhair	$40
Yorkshire Terrier	$38	Pug	$30
Cairn Terrier	$40	Beagle	$40
West Highland Terrier	$40	Bassett Hound	$45
Scottish Terrier	$45	Dalmation	$45
Wirehaired Fox Terrier	$45	Bulldog	$45
Soft-coated Wheaten	$55	Bullmastiff	$50
Airedale	$75	Great Dane	$60
Lhasa Apso	$45	Pomeranian	$40
Shih Tzu	$40	Keeshond	$50
Maltese	$38	Husky	$55
Tibetan Terrier	$45	Alaskan Malamute	$55
Bearded Collie	$65	Portuguese Water Dog	$55

Cats, Longhair

Bath and brushout	$45 and up
Haircut	$60 and up

Handstripping

	$45 per hour

Additional charges:

Flea baths	$5 to $15 depending on size
Medicated baths	$5 to $15 depending on size
Teeth brushing	$5
Anal glands expelled	$5
Dematting	$35 per hour

Prices on mixed breed dogs and cats will vary according to size, coat condition, and temperament. All prices listed are base prices only. We do not quote exact prices until we examine the pet. We reserve the right to administer a flea treatment or a medicated shampoo if pet's condition warrants it. All pets must have proof of being up-to-date on vaccinations.

Nail trims

Cats	$10
Dogs	$10

For your convenience and the health and beauty of your pet, rebooking at pickup time is highly recommended.

Chris Pawlosky and other grooming pros to teach you "speed grooming" techniques and help maximize your profits. Videos of these programs are also available.

Another method of charging for grooming is to use an hourly rate no matter what breed of dog you are grooming or which additional services you provide. Some feel this is a more professional approach, and you won't be surprising clients with extra charges at pickup time. If you make a practice of evaluating each dog when it comes in for its appointment, you can give the client an idea of what that dog needs, alleviating the "sticker shock" effect when they return to pick up and pay.

Proponents of the hourly rate maintain that it's a fairer method because it allows for such factors as temperamental differences that add up to increased time on "problem" dogs. On two little poodles, for example, it takes a lot less time for one who is well behaved and cooperative than for one who fights and bites the hand that grooms it!

Never Apologize for Quality!

Pricing is determined by the value of a product or service and the costs related to producing it. However, price is not the only factor considered by clients when it comes to choosing a professional groomer. They also look for quality, expertise, dependability, dedication, professionalism, and a humane approach to animal care. Chances are that people who make a decision based on price alone will not become the mainstays of your business—they will probably jump ship the minute someone comes along to undercut you. You need to believe in yourself to command the prices that will allow you to grow and prosper in this business and provide the lifestyle you seek for yourself and your family. People do not dicker with the mechanic, the plumber, the dentist, or the hairstylist about the cost of their services, and they shouldn't do it with you.

Having been in the business as long as we have, we know many of us have difficulty asking for the prices that we deserve. We are too self-effacing, and we sell ourselves short. We virtually work like dogs throughout our careers but often end up with precious little to show for it. Maybe it's because we chose the pet grooming field based on our love for animals.

Times have changed. We are now legitimate entrepreneurs who care for pets. According to the IRS, we are all in business to make a profit. We certainly pay our share of taxes to the government based on that profit. That's how it works, and it's nothing to be ashamed of! Some folks will always try to nickel and dime you, but when you believe in yourself and have the knowledge of what it takes to run a business, you will project that confidence when pricing your services. Keep in mind that pricing also has a lot to do with perceived value. Do you really want to be known as the cheapest groomer in town? The economics of your area come into play here, but in most cases, people will pay a little more for the best. When the only question a potential client has is the price, and they don't want to know any more about your establishment, they may not be the kind of customer you want. We will politely say, "Well, I can certainly give you a ball park price, but I can guarantee you that no one will love your baby through the grooming process like we will."

Because it is your business, you will determine your prices, but bear in mind that it's easier to start out with fees that will make it worth your while. Price increases require notifying everyone in your clientele as well as changing some of your litera-ture. So it's wise to put a great deal of thought into what you will charge for your services. Realistically, you should increase your prices on an annual basis to keep pace with the increased costs of overhead and supplies.

Oftentimes, we are put in the position to justify our prices, which can be very uncomfortable. Hold steady in your belief that your services are worth every penny that you ask, and simply state that this is the price. When is the last time you asked your lawyer or accountant to justify their fees, never mind the fellas on Wall Street? Just because you're choosing to do something you love doesn't mean you should struggle financially. Quite the contrary, and when you turn out fantastic work day after day, they'll stop asking.

It took lots of time and training for you to gain your knowledge, your "groomer's intellectual property," if you will. It's really not necessary to get into one of these tit-for-tat arguments. Instead, you may politely explain that these are the fees you charge for your services and that they are justified because of the quality you pro-vide. You may remind indignant clients that all costs go up every year, including your overhead. They don't pay the same price to get a haircut, fill up the gas tank, or dine at a fine restaurant that they did five or ten years ago. You may even politely suggest that if the lower costs they are paying elsewhere are more in line with their budget, you would certainly understand.

You do not have to care for every dog in the universe. Your services are not for everyone, but that's okay. Do not get into giving price breaks— it will come back to haunt you. Most businesses increase their prices on a yearly basis. Haggling is for the flea market, not a business that is concerned with delivering the highest quality care it can provide for beloved family pets.

Should You Barter Your Services?

Bartering is one of the oldest ways of doing business. Throughout history, people and nations have traded goods for services. When cash currency became the worldwide standard, this system fell out of favor, but with the introduction of computer networks, instant communication, and modern record-keeping systems, it is reemerging in the business marketplace, growing by leaps and bounds every year.

As a pet grooming provider, you could barter your services for any number of goods and services from other merchants, both within your community and nationally as part of a barter service network. For a small transaction fee, members of these networks become eligible to swap services and goods through classified ads in newsletters or online. The barter exchange does the record keeping for you. It keeps track of your "trade credits" (the cash value of what you barter, usually one dollar per credit) in your account. These credits are used just like cash to make transactions. For example, you could spend those credits on landscaping services from the firm down the street or save them up to take a Caribbean cruise.

There are now more than 600 barter exchange clubs operating nationwide. As barter networks begin to flourish online, they are actually becoming more affordable. Like trading stocks, when you eliminate the middleman—the broker—you can save as much as 60 percent by making your own trades online. Look into www.ubarter.com, where you can barter everything from a villa rental in Jamaica to Nascar tickets or water filtration systems. The International Reciprocal Trade Association (IRTA) estimates that in 2008 in the United States alone, more than 250,000 businesses utilized barter transactions for more than $12 billion in exchanged revenue.

Before you join a barter exchange network, you should do your homework. Don't forget that once you affiliate with it, you will be putting the reputation of your business on the line as well as your trading credits. Some questions you should ask:

- How large is the network, and how long has it been in business? (If the exchange folds, you could be out a lot of hard work and money.)
- What categories of goods and services are available? (If you can't find something you want to spend those credits on, they won't be of much value.)
- Does it offer references? (Contact some current members to see if they are happy with its services.)

At year's end, your barter exchange should provide you with a 1099 form showing the value of any services or goods you received during the year. The IRS will also be sent a copy.

You need not join a barter exchange to engage in this method of doing business. If you choose to barter on your own, however, the IRS requires that you keep records and list the fair market value of all goods and services as income. You may deduct any costs you incurred to perform the work that was bartered. To find out more, log on to the IRS site at www.irs.org. You may request Publication 525, Taxable and Nontaxable Income, which may also be downloaded from this site.

Gift Certificates

In the pet grooming industry, selling gift certificates for your services is a great idea. More than ever, it seems, people struggle to come up with ideas on what to buy for "the person who has everything." Often, that person is a retired parent or busy career professional who gets harder to buy for every year when holidays, birthdays, or anniversaries roll around. You know their pets are dear to their hearts. What could be more thoughtful than a day of beauty for Buffy at the grooming salon?

Blank certificates are available at stationery supply stores and are printed in duplicate. The purchaser gets the top copy, and the seller keeps the carbon for verification when it is redeemed. You could also produce your own version on your computer with a program such as Microsoft Publisher, embellishing it with some pet-related clip art. VistaPrint (www.vistaprint.com) has great templates for pet services already on their site and it is very user-friendly.

The next thing you need to do is let people know about it. Post one of your gift certificates right at the check-out counter. It just may provide the perfect answer for the harried shopper, and it won't even require wrapping paper or a fancy gift box!

Advertising

The purpose of advertising is to sell products or services. Manufacturers use it to convince us we need their products. If we buy a certain brand of shampoo, we will become irresistible! Companies rely on advertising to create a favorable image. It plays a key role as businesses compete for the consumer's dollar. In 2007, spending on advertising was estimated at more than $150 billion in the United States and $385 billion worldwide. Advertising your services will be a critical factor in the success of your business, playing a big part in your marketing plan. You can be the best groomer in the world, but if you keep it a secret, you won't be in business for long. Think of the service you wish to provide as a product. Who will be interested in buying it and why? How will you reach these folks to let them know you have arrived on the scene?

Internet presence is the most important media advertising you can do today. By 2011, United States companies are expected to spend $26 billion on Internet classifieds alone. While people still read their local papers and refer to their phone books on occasion, the majority of people who are looking for businesses now turn to their computer and the World Wide Web. Study after study shows that newspaper readership is down, especially since many papers have an online edition. Additionally, all you need to do to see how the traditional phone book is doing is to look at the most recent edition. Those books are getting smaller and smaller. Many of the "local" phone books have disappeared in recent years. Business owners have only so much money to go around in this new market, and the return on Internet advertising is far more successful. We ask every new customer where they heard about us and the top three answers are that they were referred by a friend, referred by veterinarian or other pet grooming pro, or they found us on the Internet. It's been ages since someone responded that they saw us in the phone book.

The importance of a great website cannot be overstated. You don't have to spend a fortune on a website, and there are many online sites where you can utilize a template to develop your own. Many are free or very reasonable and take you step-by-step through the process. A great website is not determined by how much you spend on it, but rather on how it makes a customer feel about doing business with you. And more importantly, could they find you in the first place?

Let's start with how your new customers will find you on the Internet. A person sits down at his computer and Googles "dog grooming" and "your town." If you are the only game in town this should be easy, right? Not always. The way that search engines identify websites depends on a number of factors. Entire companies are dedicated to this and this alone. They are hired to maximize a business's placement in Google and other search engines, a service called "SEO," or search engine optimization. Much of what they do is quite complicated for the lay person, but in the end the strategy to being found on the Internet is having the correct titles tags with key phrases on your pages, your phone number in a text format the search engines can read, well written and relevant text, and inbound links where you "link" with other trusted sources. Larger mass market pet supply businesses that offer grooming utilize SEO services. Even if they are ten or fifteen miles away, they will often appear on the search results long before your small business, unless you optimize your placement. The good news is that Yahoo Small Business and other website developers for small businesses consider SEO when they help you set up your site. As your business grows, you can hire an SEO company to help further develop and maximize

Social Networking and Your Business

Another aspect of the Internet and new technologies is social networking. You all know Facebook, YouTube, and Twitter, and there are new networks popping up all the time. Businesses are utilizing these media for advertising and promotion.

We have a Facebook page for our business that features photos and current information about events and our staff, and our customers become fans of our business. Once they hit the "I Like" icon on our page, they are notified every time we update our Facebook page. We post information on a variety of topics related to our business, whether it's tips for maintaining the pet's coat between grooms or summer safety recommendations. We aim to entertain and inform. The immediacy of this tool is amazing; sometimes we receive responses from our "fans" within minutes of posting.

Nothing, however, is as immediate as Twitter. Twitter is a social network where you "tweet" a short message of up to 140 characters and post it to your "followers." Some Hollywood celebrities have millions of followers, whereas a local business may have hundreds or thousands. Twitter is very hot and quite addictive. Tweeting does require a commitment, however, because it is an immediate media; if you stop being active, you will not be followed. Many pet pros use Twitter by tweeting a short blurb about an issue, event, or product that will contain a link to a larger blog or website. Social network content does tend to be useful and not simply promotional. People aren't really interested in an advertisement posted to a network, but they may be interested in a "Tips For Your New Puppy" link that leads them to your blog or website.

Social networking is essentially free if you already have a computer or smart phone that handles the Internet. It requires primarily a commitment of time to keep your content fresh and your fans and followers curious.

your web production. We have had satisfying results with Yahoo, and we resubmit our website and update our content regularly to stay current and relevant on the search engines.

Advertising in mass media such as metropolitan daily newspapers, TV, and radio is generally geared to businesses that have a broad target audience and a big advertising budget. Home-based service businesses usually have a more tightly targeted audience and limited resources. Where will you begin?

First of all, network and get those brochures and business cards out to your fellow pet grooming professionals. Once you are a known commodity in the pet grooming community, these referrals will be your lifeline. Are there dog parks in your area? This is a great place to meet and introduce yourself to people that truly take time to make their pets happy. These people are generally great customers. There is nothing better than a one-on-one interchange to connect with a potential customer.

Direct mail is another option. For a small fee you can get the list of all owners of licensed dogs in your town and neighboring communities from the town clerk's office. These mailing lists are also offered by newspapers and periodicals directly marketing to new homeowners. You often can receive the mailing lists of these fresh customers if you advertise in their paper. It's very effective when you are announcing your business opening because you know you are reaching your target market. The rising cost of postage, however, has turned this into a fairly expensive proposition.

It is not a good idea to hand deliver flyers advertising your business. Stuffing mailboxes without paying for postage is a crime and an intrusion upon the sanctuary of a person's home. Papering auto windshields at the shopping mall presents a nuisance to drivers. It's a lot of work, it can get you in trouble with mall security, and it does not create a favorable impression of your services.

No matter how small your town, you should have an ad announcing your grand opening in your local weekly newspaper. For your business this is your official birth announcement, and it's a matter of pride. The cost will depend on how large an ad you choose to run and how many times it will be published. Once your business is familiar to your hometown residents, placing an ad in a regional weekly that is delivered free to all residents is a better long-term vehicle for you. One factor affecting the price is size: To get noticed, consider an ad that is at least one column across by 2 inches down or two columns across by 2 inches down. The paper's circulation and the length of the contract you agree to will also determine the cost.

Include some pet-related artwork in your ad and a slogan if you have one: "Expert Grooming with a Loving Touch," "Loving Care for Your Pampered Pet." Consider the picture your words will paint and deliver your message in as few words as possible. "Warm and fuzzy" is good—it's reassuring to the pet owner.

One of our most successful newspaper ads informs people about "Baby's First Bath." The *baby*, in this case, is their new puppy. If it's between four and five months of age and has had its second series of shots, the first visit for a bath and nail clipping is on the house. This "freebie" acquaints the pup with the grooming process and brings its owner into our establishment. It's a chance for everyone to bond, and those who take us up on the offer usually become our customers for grooming and pet supplies. But it's that little cartoon drawing of a pup floating in a tub of bubbles and the word *baby* that catches a prospective client's eye.

We are giving owners permission to dote on their pets just as they would a human baby, telling them we are just as loving as they are and even a bit silly ourselves. Our words are tuned in to their sense of fun. Words also instill confidence: "Celebrating Forty Years of Caring for Pets and the People They Own." If you have achieved any form of certification or belong to a professional organization in your industry, your ad should include that information as well.

Ads in large metropolitan dailies are usually too costly and aimed at too wide an audience for a local pet groomer, but occasionally they offer deals for specific types of businesses. A special section is included in the newspaper (usually on a weekend) where your ad will be featured along with other pet-related firms at a reduced rate. If you enter into a contract agreeing to advertise in this type of promotion a few times a year, you can also get a sizable discount.

Big-city radio and television stations are also aimed at a mass audience and not really suitable to our needs, but local cable TV is becoming more popular among small businesses seeking to publicize their services. While thirty seconds on network TV could cost thousands of dollars, thirty-second daily "spots" on local cable are far more affordable. In AT&T-Broadband's Cape Cod zone in Massachusetts, for instance, such advertising is offered on three tiers, the most popular of which airs your ad locally on CNN, ESPN, Lifetime, USA, Nickelodeon, A&E, Discovery, TNT, TNN, and HGTV.

Your contract can be customized to fit your needs. In our area, for example, Boston Comcast Spotlight offers forty-two networks and more than 6,000 rates, allowing businesses to access the power of TV on a local level as they select cable stations fitting their target customer base within six-town zones. A few years ago, we ran a series of spots using some of our furry clients as models. They were a big hit. For such ads, a copywriter creates a script and storyboard outlining the various shots and action involved in your TV commercial. Creative touches such as computer animation that makes it look like the dogs and cats are talking or singing can add a fun touch. Call your cable company and ask for the advertising division to find out how you and your furry friends can have a shot at stardom.

One of the Locals

There are also some fairly inexpensive ways to make your presence known, such as having your logo, business name, and phone number on your vehicle as you drive around town. Magnetic signs are one option. Personalized license plates provide another way to publicize your services. Just don't get nervous when people follow you to ask about your vanity plate!

Have some T-shirts made up to turn yourself, your friends, and family members into walking billboards for your business. You could even sell them to your clients. Have a plastic badge made up with your name and business logo on it and wear it every day—at the supermarket, at the post office, and in line at the bank. People will notice and ask about what you do.

Purchase space in your church bulletin, local theater production program, high school sports schedule, Junior League newsletter, or kennel club publication. Hang flyers with tear-off strips at the supermarket, senior citizen center, skating rink, hospital, feed and grain store, bookstore, coffeehouse, or on any community bulletin board. You can print these out on your computer using any publishing program. Never leave home without a supply of business cards. It's amazing how many people you meet who love to talk about their pets! Join a "lead group" with other business professionals in your area who hold social gatherings periodically to network and swap business leads.

Donate gift certificates to area church and civic groups or specific fund-raising drives. You will get free advertising, and the winner may become a regular customer.

Do be cautious about donations to any charitable organizations though, especially those who solicit you over the phone. In our years of operation, we have had hundreds of people soliciting our contributions. An amazing number of them were scams, including some posing as support groups for law enforcement or the elderly. Tell them you need to contact your local police department or the Better Business Bureau before you give any donations. Ask them to mail you their literature because you do not take such calls on your business phone. Or tell them your advertising budget has been depleted for the year. Wish them a pleasant day and hang up.

With all these options vying for your advertising dollar, the choice can be a tough one. Remember that every advertisement is a legitimate business deduction, but don't spread yourself too thin. You can't afford to overspend your precious startup capital. After you've made your advertising choices, find out which ones work best for you. When you meet a new client, always ask, "How did you find out about our services?"

Networking and Petworking: Referrals Mean Business!

In the pet grooming field, networking—or, in our field, petworking—is vital to your success. Referrals from other pet grooming professionals provide positive results for all concerned. The vet is happy that he or she can refer the matted little shih tzu's owner to professionals who know what they are doing and who run a clean, safe grooming shop; the groomer recommends a pet sitter to a client who must leave town on short notice and has no one to take care of little Fifi; the trainer will be pleased to work with that grumpy little cocker who thinks its groomer's arm is a chew toy. In our business, what goes around comes around.

Contacts like these don't come out of the blue. You need to nourish them and feed them. Your vet—and more importantly, his or her technicians—will not feel comfortable handing out your cards unless you are a known entity. Before you set up your business, you should always make the rounds of vets, trainers, pet shops, kennels, groomers, and shelters—in short, anyone who works with animals who could recommend your services.

This does not mean dumping a bunch of business cards on the counter and bolting for the door. You need to establish a personal relationship. When you first met with that local vet, unless you were already a client, you should have made an appointment—and paid for it.

Meet with shelter personnel and see if there is any way you can help out, possibly by offering a free grooming to unkempt potential adoptees. Place shelter canisters in prominent places in your shop to help collect donations. Donate damaged items or out-of-code pet foods to these needy pets. Send over a basket of cookies or catnip treats at holiday time or a box of chocolates to the hardworking volunteers on Valentine's Day.

Once you have become a success in your community, it is extremely gratifying to help another pet grooming provider get started. You have no idea of the power you wield once the public puts its trust in you. In this business, which is, after all, based on love for our pets, there really is room for us all.

Word of Mouth: Still the Best

After all is said and done, word of mouth still works best when it comes to advertising pet grooming services. If you benefit from it, return the favor. When one of your loyal customers sends you a new client, reward the referral with a discounted grooming. Most important: Keep doing a great job so your clients will keep coming back and sending their friends as well.

Public Relations: Tooting Your Own Horn

The squeaky wheel gets the grease. That's another one of those old sayings we've all heard too many times. But when it comes to promoting your pet grooming business, it expresses an important truth. In your small business, you wear all the hats, including that of Director of Public Relations. By now you've pretty much decided where you will spend your initial advertising dollars, but when it comes to PR, guess what? Besides your time, imagination, and the cost of paper and ink, you can do it for nothing! Virtually everything you do can be turned into a PR opportunity. You just need to decide which venues you will use to get the word out about your services, your accomplishments, and what makes you unique.

News Releases

A news release is nothing more than an advertisement you don't have to pay for. Every business has numerous opportunities to send out these image-enhancing messages. In the pet grooming business, we are more fortunate than most because all newspapers periodically feel the need to run appealing stories related to animals, especially if accompanied by an irresistible picture. It's like those typical summer shots you see every July: the bathing beauty at the beach or the kid eating an ice-cream cone. You've seen them countless times before, but you're still compelled to look!

Begin your foray into publicizing yourself by compiling a list of local and regional newspapers, noting the name, address, and editor of each. Add the phone number, too, as you may need to contact the editor if your release doesn't get into print in a timely manner. Always be courteous when you call to inquire about whether an editor plans to run your news release. This is strictly an editorial decision—you don't want to burn your bridges by acting as if it was an announcement from the White House! Newspapers are bombarded with news releases every day, and the volume of news they need to print also affects what they will use. News releases are considered "filler": They can run them today or save them until next week. If you do make a follow-up call, ask the editor if more information is needed. You may even get lucky and have this contact lead to an interview and a feature story about you and your business.

Your first news release can be about your grand opening. You could send it out on your business letterhead, or even better, e-mail it directly to the editor, but be sure to include your name as the contact person in case a follow-up is needed for clarification or additional information. Designate it "For Immediate Release," and print the headline in capital letters. Attach a shot of yourself with a pet or pets, if you have one. The first paragraph should provide a brief summary, answering the standard reporter's questions: who, what, when, where, why, and how. This "lead" should be punchy enough to capture the readers' interest, compelling them to read the entire article. State the information as briefly as you can—most newspapers have tight requirements when it comes to space. Make sure it's typed, double spaced, and dated for immediate release.

At the end of your release, type in "-30-" or "END," centered, after your last paragraph. Before you e-mail or mail it off to the newspaper office, addressed to the editor by name, be sure to proofread it to check for spelling errors.

If you win an award, publicize it—PR opportunities just don't get any better than that! Here is a typical release based on a groomer's first grooming competition win. Ideally, it would be accompanied by a professional photo taken at the show.

Other events worthy of a news release include hiring a new employee, expanding your business, adding a new service, volunteer activities (especially those related

Contact: **For Immediate Release**

Mary Jones

(508) 555–2240

SISTERS DELIVER PURR-FECT PET CARE TO YOUR HOME

PLAINFIELD, MA—Sisters Mary Jones and Judy Black have turned their love for pets into a new business venture. Starting April 1, they will be making the rounds in Plainfield, East Greenville, and Johnstown, providing mobile grooming for all manner of creatures. Jones and Black describe their business as an alternative for many pet owners, including the elderly and those with disabilities, who have trouble transporting their pet to the grooming salon. It is also ideal for the pet owner whose pet suffers from travel anxiety. For them, having a grooming shop on wheels roll right into the driveway to provide grooming for their pets is just what the doctor ordered.

"Our mobile grooming service has all the luxuries of a full-service pet spa," says Jones. "We use state-of-the-art grooming equipment and offer a peaceful and serene environment for any pet right outside his front door."

Both women are avid pet lovers. Black and her golden retriever, Mandy, are familiar faces at the Shady Hill Retirement Home as they make weekly pet therapy visits to senior citizens. Jones is a well-known breeder of Himalayan cats, and her MoonMist Cattery has produced several champions. Because both women have growing families, their new business will allow them to make their own hours. "Our husbands think it's great," Jones says. "As long as we promise not to bring home any of our furry clients!"

The sisters are members of the National Dog Groomers Association of America (NDGAA), an organization for professional pet groomers. To find out more, pet owners should call them at (508) 555–2240 or (508) 555–4267. Before booking their services, they will make a visit to discuss special needs and get acquainted with the pets.

END

Contact: **For Immediate Release**
Jane Smith
(508) 555–2345

LOCAL GROOMER WINS AWARD

PLAINFIELD, MA—Professional pet groomer Jane Smith of Fur Magnolias Grooming Salon brought home the glory last weekend with her first grooming competition win at the New England Pet Grooming Professionals Fall Festival held in Sturbridge, Massachusetts. She received first prize in the toy and miniature poodles division with Coquette, a black miniature poodle owned by client Arthur Rogers of Johnstown. As a novice, she competed in the "B" division against a field of twelve other groomers.

Smith was awarded $100 plus a trophy, ribbons, and assorted merchandise for her salon. "It was a great experience and a chance to sharpen my skills," she said. "I loved the challenge of competing. I learned a lot, and I will definitely return to the contest ring to compete again!"

END

to pets), attendance at industry conventions, or gaining certification or accreditation in your field.

All the World's a Stage: Special Events

Special events are also newsworthy. If you hold a Halloween costume party for dogs at your grooming shop or plan a photo shoot with Santa Claus, get the word out to the media beforehand to line up coverage. If proceeds from any such event, in part or in full, go to charity, that's frosting on the cake!

Any event you hold for charity should draw media interest. A bake sale including cookies from the new doggie bakery to benefit the shelter, a dog walk at a local park to raise funds for the humane society or a spay/neuter fund, a day of beauty for the shelter with grooming services donated to spruce up adoptable pets, a flea market for a pet-related charity, or a block party for people and their pets in your parking lot or in a local park (with official permission, of course)—these are public relations stories waiting to happen.

Your outdoor event could feature an obedience training exercise or police dog demonstration, an agility demonstration, a "freestyle" exhibition of people dancing with their dogs, or a cart-pulling event. We held such a block party to commemorate the birthday of Missi's toy poodle, Mookie, our beloved shop mascot, complete with balloon animals, clowns, pony rides, refreshments, and a "Moon Walk" for kids. All proceeds from Mookie's party were donated to charity. Fun events such as these draw media coverage from newspapers and TV stations, making your presence known in the community. They offer a great chance for informal camaraderie with your clientele, and they raise funds for animal-related causes. Granted, planning and hosting them takes a good deal of effort, but the work you put into them will pay off in a public relations bonanza for you and your business.

Your news release can also announce your presence as you host a booth at someone else's fund-raiser. We manned a nail-trimming booth to collect donations for a pet walk hosted by a local shelter and offered a table of pet-related items at another's fair and flea market on the town common. Such "petworking" opportunities strengthen your connections to your fellow pet grooming professionals. Refer people to them just as they refer people to you, keeping a ready supply of their business cards on hand for your clients.

If there is an indoor pet fair in your community or if your local chamber of commerce holds a trade show, consider renting a booth. You could cut the cost by splitting the rental with another pet grooming provider, each using half the space. Usually, event promoters provide table skirts and electricity for each booth. If you have a small TV/VCR, you could run educational information videos. If you have been a guest on a local cable show, the tape they normally give you would be perfect. Bring plenty of cards and brochures. Of course, having some cute pets in attendance is a natural draw.

Have a drawing for free services or a pet-related prize. Use a fishbowl to collect the names and addresses of all who take part in your drawing. Offer refreshments such as candy or cookies for browsers. Have pictures of your furry clients on display. Your participation will identify you as a professional, and you'll have a good time in the process.

For a Good Cause: How to Be Both Charitable and Wise

You will no doubt be astonished by all the requests that come your way for donations to civic groups, youth sports teams, school fairs, churches, and so on. One way to be generous and publicize your business in the process is by donating gift certificates for a free grooming with the dollar amount spelled out by you. Along with your donation, you will receive free advertising and the added goodwill of helping out in your community. We've gotten some wonderful grooming clients this way. In addition, your donation can be written off as a legitimate business expense. Don't go overboard and give away the store. If you have any questions about the legitimacy of a charitable request or organization, check it out with local law enforcement before you agree to donate any of your hard-earned money.

Sharing Your Knowledge

When it comes to questions about pets and their care, you're a natural. You will be amazed at the number of times you will be asked how to crate-train a puppy, what kind of treats are safe to give a pet, which dog food to use, and how to correct a pet's annoying habits. It's wonderful to be thought of as a resource in your community, and you should make the most of it.

To polish up this image even further, contact your local cable TV or radio station to see if you could be a guest to talk about pets and their care. You could also prepare a resume of your credentials to introduce yourself to these media outlets for future reference. We have done several shows about grooming and pet grooming careers on our local cable station. When summer rolls around, a reporter calls or shows up to interview us about hot-weather safety tips. At holiday time, we are called upon to discuss seasonal do's and don'ts for pets.

Your local newspaper may welcome a column about such pet-related topics. If you have a talent for self-expression, write one up and submit it to the editor. Whether or not you get paid for it is irrelevant—you will be getting your name out there as an expert in your field.

When folks are looking for a puppy or an older dog to adopt, they often come to us for the names of breeders or breed rescue groups. They ask about the traits of a particular breed and whether it would be a good choice for their lifestyle. They want to know who we recommend when their pet needs a veterinary specialist for orthopedic work or vision problems, or if we know of an inn on Cape Cod where dogs are welcome.

Making yourself into a community resource is incredibly rewarding. It's great to be able to tell people about your fellow professionals: the trainer who offers puppy kindergarten classes, the pet sitter who will make midday visits to give medication to a canine senior citizen. Helping people and their pets is one of the biggest perks of a pet grooming career.

You can also share your expertise and the joys of pet ownership with the children in your community. Volunteer to speak at career days, bringing along a kid-friendly pet or two (with the school's permission, of course). Sponsor an essay contest or a drawing contest during National Pet Week in May. At Christmastime, hold a "Make Your Pet a Stocking Day" for kids at your grooming salon. The possibilities for creating fun events that also publicize your business will be limited only by your imagination!

Public Speaking

For some of us, just the thought of getting up to speak in front of a group of people is enough to get those butterflies in the stomach ready for takeoff. In the category of stressful situations, public speaking rates right up there with divorce or death! The good news is that almost everyone can master this skill. If you can overcome your fears, it can become a great public relations tool for you and your business.

There are various ways to hone your skills in this area. In many communities, courses are offered in evening adult education programs, which are inexpensive and fun. Organizations such as Toastmasters International and the Dale Carnegie courses in leadership training exist nationwide to instruct people in this type of communicating and help build self-confidence. Check their websites (www.toast masters.org or www.dalecarnegietraining.com) for the chapter nearest you. There are also private businesses and coaches listed in the yellow pages under Public Speaking—Instructions.

In all such courses, everyone is in the same boat when it comes to being nervous, but participants are usually kind and supportive as they help each other build confidence and skills.

Speaking engagements before community groups will bring you new customers. Organizations such as the chamber of commerce, the Rotary, Kiwanis, the Lions Club, Jaycees, and local business and professional groups will provide you a venue for speaking about your services. Senior citizens and their pets share a very special life-enhancing bond, and your presentation about pet grooming at a senior center would be welcomed and appreciated. Schools and youth organizations would enjoy your talk about pets, emphasizing education on responsible care in addition to highlighting the services you provide.

Don't forget to inject some humor into your speech. If you can bring a pet or two along, so much the better—they make great ice-breakers. Use visual aids if possible, such as an overhead projector and slides or a video related to your services. Remember to bring brochures and business cards. If your audience is made up of children, advertising items such as pens, key chains, and business card magnets are always a big hit.

To increase your comfort level, practice with family and friends first and ask for an honest critique. When you speak in public, it helps if you visualize yourself telling your story to a friend. Learn to smile and make eye contact—nothing is more boring than a person who steps up to the podium and simply reads a prepared speech. Most folks in your audience will be very supportive and kind and will be genuinely interested in the information you are providing. Invite their questions when you are through. Don't forget, when they get up to speak, they probably get butterflies, too!

Your Personal Pipeline: Publishing a Newsletter or Ezine

If you can use a computer, you can publish a newsletter or e-mail an Ezine. Programs such as Microsoft Publisher or any desktop publishing software will walk you through the process, customizing your layout, fonts, clip art, and columns as well as answering any questions that may crop up in the process.

A newsletter is a great image builder as well as an advertising tool. It adds a new level of professionalism to your business services. What will your newsletter have to say? We typically cover any newsworthy items since our last publication, and then offer up useful information for the current season. We also write at least one human interest story about a dog we care for or an amusing story from the past few months. We always feature "Up in Heaven Barking" to pay tribute to pets we've lost since our last edition. News about our own continuing education or a staff member's attendance to a trade show is also an image booster for a newsletter.

Any previously published material you wish to use, including cartoons, may be used only with the permission of the publication from which they came. Plagiarism and copyright infringement are against the law and should be taken very seriously. Most trade journals, pet-related websites, and veterinary school publications will be happy to give you permission to use such information.

You can use your newsletter to announce special promotions or memorialize beloved pets or their owners who have passed on. You can share a humorous anecdote about one of your own pets or a four-legged customer, or write about a client, telling about a recent trip, job, or activity—everyone loves those fifteen minutes of fame. You may include letters from clients or help-wanted ads. No matter what information you choose to impart, keep it light and avoid getting up on your soapbox unless the issue concerns the welfare of pets.

You can print your newsletters yourself or take the original to the local printer, where they will turn them out for pennies per copy. Mailing them is another matter. Depending on how many pieces and how often you plan to publish, a bulk mail permit from the post office will usually cost between $150 and $200, a fee that must be paid annually. The cost varies according to the number of pieces, and you can get a discount by sorting them according to zip code. To obtain such a permit, you must send at least 200 pieces or fifty pounds of mail.

Another alternative is to have a mailing company such as the UPS Store or Mail Boxes Etc. handle the mailing for you. Not all franchisees do it, so call ahead to check. The ones that do will take your copy either on paper or on disk, then print, tabulate, address, and sort your newsletters according to zip code. (They actually add a bar code, which automates the mailing for the post office.) An average run of 1,000 pieces may cost you up to 50 cents per piece, but you would save on postage, making the process more affordable.

Some businesses offset the cost of their newsletters by offering advertising space to other businesses or organizations. With enough advertisers, you might even turn a profit. Pet food companies, vets, other animal-related businesses, pet supply stores—all would be good places to start looking for "patrons." They may even distribute the newsletters in their places of business. Only you can decide if the amount you will spend on a printed newsletter will generate enough business to make it worth your while.

There are alternatives to mailing a newsletter, the most modern of which is publishing yours online. Have your clients sign up by giving you their e-mail addresses. If you have a website, be sure to include a link to your newsletters. We e-mail our newsletter, but we still offer copies to our customers on our countertop as well. They disappear like hotcakes! How you distribute your particular newsletter will depend on your business and your costs, but it's a great way to communicate with your clients and polish your image in the process.

Check Us Out on the Web!

In 1984 there were 300 Internet users. There are now more than 260 million in North America and an estimated 1.8 billion worldwide. Internet growth has exploded in a whole new universe of communication.

Online shopping is becoming more and more commonplace. In the United States online shoppers are expected to reach 132 million in the next five years. With today's hectic schedules, people need a way to save time, and shopping online is a way to do this. A recent study found that 19 percent of Internet users shop online once per week, and this number will continue to grow.

So why should you have a website? Because everybody else does? Well, yes. It gives you a distinctive presence and identifies you as an up-to-date member of the business community. By visiting your site, your clients can get information about your services from the comfort of their homes. You can explain everything they need to know: policies, background, history, and prices.

Our site, www.villagegroomer.net, features biographical information, pictures of our canine and feline clients and family members, a menu of services, tribute pages for pets who have passed away, a link to our sister business, Dog Daze Day Camp, plus links to our published writings. The site also provides links to the American Kennel Club, local humane shelters and rescue groups, pet sitting services, our on-staff obedience trainer, the Pet Loss Grief Support Network, and copyrighted material from pet food companies whose products we feature in our store, used, of course, with their permission.

A website provides a wonderful introduction to your services. Make sure you list your web address on all of your advertising, including signage on your vehicle, business cards, and brochures. Because the Internet is open 24 hours a day, seven days a week, your website never closes. For web surfers, it's only a click away.

Advertising and Promotion Checklist

		Completed
1.	Write your own bio story and announce the opening of your business as a news release for your local and regional newspapers.	❑
2.	Volunteer to give a talk on pet grooming at local schools as part of career day presentations.	❑
3.	Look for business organizations in order to meet new people and publicize your services in the community.	❑
4.	Volunteer to do a grooming demonstration at your community's annual fair.	❑
5.	Volunteer to host a nail-cutting booth at the local humane society's annual fund-raising dog walk.	❑
6.	Volunteer to donate a free grooming to shelter pets who need it to make them more adoptable.	❑
7.	Publish a shop newsletter giving seasonal pet health and safety tips and news items regarding yourself and your clients.	❑

8. Decide how to best set up your website. ❐

   Register your domain name. ❐

   Call your current ISP and other hosts to compare
   web-hosting rates. ❐

   Decide whether to use a fee-based or a no-fee hosting service. ❐

   Decide if you will hire a professional website designer, or
   research appropriate Internet software and Web design
   courses at the local community college or adult education
   courses at the local high school. ❐

   Decide how you want your site to look—pictures, text,
   content—and the number of pages you will require.
   (Hint: Consider hiring a high school or college student to
   help design your site.) ❐

9. Investigate the cost of installing a toll-free phone
   number. ❐

10. Request catalogs from companies specializing in
    promotional products such as bumper stickers, pens,
    magnets, key chains, and calendars. Identify items you
    can use and afford to best promote your services. ❐

The Personal Touch

Among the joys of a pet grooming career are the personal bonds you forge with clients and their beloved pets. In this line of work, you automatically gain admission to a private world where not many people are invited to visit. This happens because people trust you. Otherwise, they would not seek out your services to care for their "surrogate children." If this is your calling, then along with the grooming services you provide, you will also be delivering loving care and peace of mind.

Our founder, David Salzberg, was a great animal lover. He had unlimited patience and found joy in even the shaggiest beast that came into our shop. The love he projected was one of the things that helped our business to succeed. In fact, we believe that in their heart of hearts, every pet-owning client harbored their own precious little secret: They were sure that of all the animals that came to the Village Groomer, Dave loved theirs the best!

When Work and Play Are One

Does this sound like deception? It shouldn't. Caring for animals is not a cold and mechanical job. If you don't love them, you won't enjoy it. Eventually, they will get on your nerves and leave you wondering whatever made you decide to do this for a living. Opening up your heart to the love and appreciation of your furry clients will do wonders for you and your business. It will keep your phone ringing and make you more successful.

Many midlifers and downsized nine-to-fivers enter the world of pet grooming because it offers something different, outside the mainstream of the buttoned-down corporate world. It's a way of living that allows us to have fun. It is said that people who can combine work and play are the happiest of all. They are getting paid for doing something they love. Some of us have learned along the way that even if we were making a lot of money, if we dreaded going to work every day, the paycheck was not enough. You can be rich and still be miserable. The pet grooming career path offers us loving interactions—and fun—each and every day.

Share this attitude of play with your coworkers and your clients. Have a sense of playfulness, a special little nickname for each pet, an anecdote to share at the end of the day. When reminiscing about our founder, Dave, one prim and proper matron tearfully confided that it always tickled her funny bone when he called her chubby cocker spaniel "Chunky Chicken." We are always trying to bring a smile to someone's face. When a baby bonnet in our lost and found box went unclaimed, we started using it as a playful prop. If any of our employees are having a tough day or just feeling sorry for themselves, we give them the "baby hat" to lighten things up. It brings a laugh because it is done with love.

One of the reasons that people have pets is to relieve the stress of the workaday world. In your pet grooming business, your welcoming presence gives them permission to be silly, to let their tender feelings show. This business is all about personal interaction. Develop the skill of really listening to your clients. This will help you to take better care of their needs and the needs of their pets. You will get to know these folks well in the process. They are the ones who are paying your bills, putting the groceries on the table, and helping to pay for your son's braces. Developing a personal relationship will keep them coming back. Just like at Cheers, that homey Boston bar made famous on TV, those regulars kept coming back because it was a place "where everybody knows your name"—and we even know their pets' names, too!

Beyond doing a good job of caring for your clients' pets, there are other ways to enhance the personal touch. If a client is ill, send a get-well card (with animals on it, of course). In times of loss, attend their services and send a sympathy card or spiritual bouquet. Make a memorial donation to the loved one's favorite charity. If they need to get the dog groomed or require pet sitting services at the time of bereavement, offering to take care of them without charging for your services is a caring touch that will always be remembered.

If there's a wedding coming up for one of your customers, match the color of Buffy's bows to the bridesmaids' dresses. Give a little stuffed dog or cat when a client has a baby. If you sell retail products, take the time to show clients something that will interest them: "I was thinking of you when I picked up this item." Gestures like this cement the personal bond between you and your clients.

Sweet Remembrance: Seasonal Gifts for Your Customers

The holidays offer a whole new opportunity to say thanks to your loyal customers. Some pet grooming people send out personalized holiday cards, featuring a picture of them with their pets and a hand-written message of goodwill and thanks. Every year, Village Groomer clients look forward to our calendars, which feature pictures of adorable pets, of course. As for their animals, we always give out little boxes of holiday-specific cookies. If you sell pet treats, you may be able to get them in individual-size gift packaging. You could also do a search for "dog bakeries" on the Internet. You'll come up with hundreds of businesses, many of them near you.

Don't forget the diversity of your client base when it comes to holiday gifts and items for sale. Not everyone celebrates Christmas. Get out your calendar and make yourself aware of the dates for Hanukkah and Kwanzaa. Our "cookie man" provides us with brightly colored plastic dreidels filled with treats for our Jewish clients. Our gift cookie boxes bear the message "Happy Holidays" rather than "Merry Christmas."

Our groomers go into a bow-making frenzy using Christmas and Hanukkah ribbon, curling ribbon, and jingle bells as they adorn each and every pet with a holiday bow. Some pet grooming providers use bandanas instead. Most pet supply houses offer them for every holiday, along with a huge variety of ribbons. Instead of cookies, you can give each pet an inexpensive toy, bought in bulk and completely deductible, of course. For dogs, it might be a squeaky toy; for cats, a catnip pillow or furry mouse with a holiday ribbon. You can also make up your own little remembrances, a framed magnet picture of each pet, a homemade ornament, your own little bag of goodies, or some pet-related item you come across at an industry convention such as Intergroom or GroomExpo.

You may also shop for such items at a regional gift center. Now that you are in business, you will need to obtain a tax number for resale from the state allowing you to purchase from these wholesalers or attend their gift shows. They are not open to the public. Conduct an online search for gift wholesalers and shows in your area. You can't actually buy items at these wholesale centers or gift shows, but you can get a look at the products and place orders. The time to start planning how you will make the holidays a special time for you and your customers is during the summer months. By the time you get into the busy holiday season, it will be too late.

Dealing with Difficult Clients

The vast majority of your pet-owning customers will be pleasant and reasonable, but sooner or later you are bound to run across that difficult client who really tests your people skills and professionalism. It may be the woman who calls at the last minute and gets highly irate because you can't accommodate her. It may be someone who feels the need to haggle over your prices. It may come out of left field, a person who accuses you of being negligent or harming a pet in your care.

How will you handle these problem people? First and foremost, try to remain calm and professional. Every business on the planet gets complaints. Second, deal with the situation immediately. If you leave a complaint unanswered, it will only add to your stress level and the unhappy client's indignation. The person who comes at you all puffed up and ready to do battle can usually be defused by a calm and understanding approach. Before you offer any remedy, listen to what the person has to say.

Communicating Clearly

Most client problems revolve around the issue of communication. If you think the complaint has any merit, ask what the client thinks you could do to correct the situation. If it's a misunderstanding about a grooming style ("You clipped Muffy's head way too short, and I told you not to trim her ears"), and if you want to keep that person as a client, offer the next visit at a reduced fee or free of charge. Compensating for a client's disappointment with a future free or discounted service is far superior to refunding the person's money. Whether they were pleased with the results or not, you performed the service in good faith. If it is something you can correct about the grooming job then and there, by all means do it while the client waits.

In a busy grooming shop, things can get hectic at intake time. The best way to avoid such miscommunication is to go over each dog or cat to see what kind of shape it's in before agreeing to do a certain style. You cannot imagine the repercussions of agreeing to "just give him a puppy cut" as the client bolts out the door before you have had a chance to examine the coat. In our salon, we will not shave a pet down without the owner's consent, and we take great pains to explain what we mean by "stripping" a pet's coat. At best, most clients retain about a third of what you tell them. Honing your communication skills is the best way to avoid disappointing them with your work and causing an angry backlash directed at you.

In the client's eyes you are now a pet grooming expert, and an important part of your job involves client education. When a new customer comes in for an initial appointment, take the time to explain the grooming needs of the pet. Demonstrate proper brushing techniques for maintenance care between grooming appointments. A cautionary note: If you use groomer jargon and fail to fully explain your terminology, the person could be too embarrassed to ask what you mean and might completely misunderstand the information.

Aggressive Pets

Sometimes clients get offended if we do not want to care for their aggressive or dangerous dogs. A dog with its neck and back hair bristling, that cowers in fear, growls, snarls, or tries to bite you, is not a safe dog to handle. If a dog shows signs of vicious behavior as you take it from its owner, do yourself a favor and do not accept that dog as a customer. As you become more familiar with dog behavior and body language, you can usually tell the ones that will pose a real threat to you or your employees. Listen to your intuition because it is almost always right! No amount of money is worth the stress and risk in grooming an animal that is out of control. Some people think that just because we work with animals, we can handle anything. They get offended when you tell them that little Spunky spent his whole grooming session trying to chew on your arm. They look at you with suspicion and wonder what you did to provoke him. Contrary to the beliefs of owners like these, pet grooming providers are not immune to injury. When we get bitten, we bleed just like everybody else.

In most cases, we can read canine or feline body language. If the animal does not calm down enough to cooperate or shows serious aggression, we make that phone call to the owner explaining that we tried but we were unable to groom the pet. On the other hand, there have been many times when we have worked successfully with grumpy or fearful pets and won them over with patience and time. This is a great ego booster, making us feel we're on a par with Dr. Dolittle!

It's an individual call, but before you agree to groom a pet that wants to eat you for lunch, remind yourself that you cannot work if you are injured. If one of your employees gets bitten, it's even worse. Not only do you feel concern for the injured worker, you also feel responsible for taking that dog as a client. In addition to the stress level such a crisis brings, you are faced with the hassle of insurance claims, workers' compensation reporting, and notifying the animal control officer, the local health department, and the pet owner. Even if the animal is up-to-date on its vaccinations, it must be quarantined for ten days after a biting incident. Then there is the added strain of working understaffed while your injured employee recuperates. When in doubt, go with your intuition. The world is full of lovely pets that will not endanger you or your staff.

There may be times when you do not discover that a pet is aggressive until you are in the middle of a grooming session. If you begin the grooming procedure and the dog proves too dangerous or difficult, place it back in the crate or cubby and call the owner to explain why you cannot complete the job. Aggressive behavior can often be corrected by an obedience trainer, and there are some trainers who specialize in handling this particular problem. You might even refer the owner to a trainer who can help, but this is not a job for a groomer.

Nonpayment for Services

Once in a while you may run into the client who refuses to pay for your services. Grooming is usually a "cash and carry" business, and most of us are not set up to do credit billing. The client pays for our services when they are performed. We have run into only one client who just plain refused to pay our price, offering only a small portion of what was due. The police were called and, once the situation was explained, she chose to ante up for the remaining amount. We were lucky in that case because it was our word against hers. Legally, we would not have been allowed to hold her pet until such time as she paid up which was fine with us, as her "baby" was a ninety-pound Samoyed!

Most unpaid bills are the results of bad checks for which you are not reimbursed. In our experience, this has happened rarely, far less often as debit card usage increases. Most such instances are the result of checking account mix-ups or people who are disorganized in handling their accounts. Be diplomatic when you call to inform a client that a check has been returned. You should have a policy requiring clients to pay any bank charges incurred by overdrafts. Most businesses also assess a fee for bounced checks, commonly ranging from $10 to $25.

If two calls from you do not result in the person coming in to make good on the check, send a letter bringing the matter to the client's attention and requesting payment within five days. Your tone should be friendly but firm, indicating the date your services were rendered, the number and date of the check that was returned, and the dates of the calls you made to the person. Your letter may state: "We enjoy grooming your pet and value you as a customer. We feel certain this matter is just an oversight on your part, but we need you to take care of it immediately so we may clear it from our books. Therefore, we thank you in advance for remitting payment for these services to us within the next five (5) days."

Helping Clients Deal with Pet Illness and Bereavement

One of the most difficult aspects about working with pets has to do with illness and bereavement. Because their expected life spans are so much shorter than ours, loving a pet brings with it a built-in heartbreak down the road. As a pet grooming provider, you will find yourself sharing in the grieving process with your clients when a beloved pet dies or when they face that difficult decision about whether it's time for euthanasia. They will count on you for support, and it really is a privilege.

   You can provide a safe and respectful place for grieving pet owners to process their loss. How heartbreaking and maddening it is to hear "It was only a dog" from somebody who just "doesn't get it." Some people have no idea what an emotional blow it can be to lose a four-legged family member. You are faced with the whole grieving process—anger, denial, acceptance, and healing—before you are able to move on. Like it or not, as a pet grooming provider you've been thrust into the role of bereavement counselor.

   Beyond a few friends and family members, who else really grieves with people who lose a pet? Who acknowledges the impact such losses have upon our lives?

You cared for their pet, and you knew its little idiosyncrasies. It's perfectly normal to share a smile at that pet's antics and shed a few tears when you comfort your grieving client. We know from experience that the first person they call when the loss occurs is often their groomer.

Beyond your words of comfort, it's nice to acknowledge the loss with a card bearing a personalized message, a bouquet or plant, or a donation to a shelter or rescue organization in the pet's name. There are pet bereavement products available, such as the Pet Memorial Candle offered by Furry Angel of California. The candleholder has a moving poem inscribed on it. The process of lighting it can be a peaceful, calming ritual for the bereaved owner. (It is also a nice item to carry if you sell pet-related retail products.) You can find the company online at www.furryangel.com, where you will also find links to other pet loss sites.

At www.petloss.com you will find the Pet Loss Grief Support website, a wonderful resource for clients who have lost a pet. It includes a link to the Rainbow Bridge (www.rainbowbridge.com), a moving and beautiful poem about the journey of our departed pets. Whether or not the afterlife is part of your belief system, it is comforting to visit this site and read the story. Its final paragraph speaks of a meeting that may await you when your own life is over:

"You have been spotted, and when you and your special friend finally meet, you cling together in joyous reunion, never to be parted again. The happy kisses rain upon your face; your hands again caress the beloved head, and you look once more into the trusting eyes of your pet, so long gone from your life but never absent from your heart."

Those visiting the site are invited to take part in the worldwide Pet Loss Candle Ceremony, visit tribute pages, read inspirational poetry and articles, participate in online chat rooms and local support groups, or receive telephone support if needed. For those whose pets are ill, there is also a link for "Special Needs Pets."

Sometimes our clients seek our advice when a pet is terminally ill or incapacitated. They are suffering with the decision of whether it's time to have the pet "put to sleep." It's an honor to be the trusted confidante they seek out at this difficult time, but the decision they will make is ultimately their own. No matter how compassionate your intention, if you are the one to advise they have the pet euthanized, you are overstepping your bounds. You could even incur their resentment or blame later on. Be there to offer your support as a listening ear for them as they wrestle with this painful decision, and extend your condolences if a client decides to let a beloved pet go to its rest.

It helps to remember your own experiences with pet loss, how necessary it was for you to take the time to be sad and grieve before you moved on. If you ever find yourself going through it again, your clients will be there for you, too.

14 Watching Baby Grow

As the pet industry grows, so does the need for pet grooming services. You may have opted to start small, running your business alone or with a partner, but within a few years, you may find yourself "maxed out" in meeting the demand for grooming. You're becoming overbooked and overworked. You may have come to a crossroads where you need to make a decision about your future growth.

This is the time to sit down with your accountant and go over your volume of business and income since you opened. Has it increased every year? Are there other factors that have impacted your business? Have any of your competitors retired or gone out of business? What about the economic health of your community? Are housing values and population figures on the rise? Now is the time to look at your pricing structure. If you are booked solid most of the time, it's time to consider raising your prices. The law of supply and demand applies to pet grooming workers, too.

Reviewing your financial records will help you set goals. Refer to your business plan to see if you have achieved any of the milestones you set for yourself back in the planning and dreaming stages. Your records will reveal the busiest and slowest times for your business. These figures will help you make the decision on whether it's time to add staff.

Your accountant's input is key in making decisions regarding your growth. Together you will crunch the numbers, looking at such considerations as starting wages you could offer, the cost of benefits, and the tax implications. Once you have employees, you must pay workers' compensation tax and withhold state, federal, and social security taxes from their paychecks.

Growth Opportunities

Hiring a bather-brusher will allow you to spend more time on your grooming and increase your productivity. Adding a receptionist, even part-time, will free-up your hands to groom more. Burnout is a recognized occupational hazard in this field. Too many of us are "people-pleasers" who regularly put our customers' needs ahead of our own.

You started your venture as a home-based business, but in some cases, you may need to leave home to grow. A commercial location will allow you to build a larger clientele. Both home groomers and mobile groomers have a built-in ceiling on how many pets they can accommodate in their limited space. In planning for your future, including retirement, you should take into account that when you own or lease a commercial property, your business will be far more attractive and worth much more to a prospective buyer.

Selling a home-based business is another matter. Unless you are selling your house and business as one, the potential buyer is faced with moving the clientele and adapting his or her own residence to suit the business. Local and state regulations that apply to home businesses grow more stringent every year. Your costs to set up your home salon were considerably less than those of your colleagues who rented commercial space, but at retirement time you will be faced with self-imposed limitations when it comes to net worth and resale value.

Adding to Your Staff

Right now you may envision your business as a one-person show, but it is quite likely that will change. As you build your clientele and your desire to work more efficiently, you will probably consider hiring employees. You might start with a bather-brusher, perhaps initially just on Saturday. Later, you may wish to add another groomer to accommodate your customers. Where in the world do you look for help?

The first thing you need to do is to check to make sure you can have employees. Some municipalities do not allow additional employees, other than family members, in a home-based business. Many small-business owners have their spouses or children pitch in as employees. If that is not an option for you and it is legal to proceed, then you need to get the word out that you are hiring.

Finding pet grooming personnel is not easy. It's not like working at the fast-food restaurant or the car wash. This field requires true animal lovers who have an abundance of kindness and compassion and are willing to work hard. They need to be dependable and trustworthy. If they will be dealing with the public, they need people skills because they will be representing you and your business. A rude or crude employee can do serious damage to the image you have worked so hard to build. Begin your search by word of mouth. Tell your clients, business associates, and friends that you are looking. Tell the woman at the coffee shop and the stylist where you get your hair done. Post a sign where all can see it. Advertise in your newsletter, on your website, and put flyers on bulletin boards at the vet's office, the kennel, the training facility, the pet supply store, and the humane shelter. Talk to your fellow merchants at the chamber of commerce.

Sometimes a friend or relative will step forward to offer their help. Although this can be a blessing, it's important to let them know that this will be a business relationship. You will not expect any less of them in handling their responsibilities because you have a personal relationship.

If you have exhausted your personal and business connections and still come up empty, it's time to place a help-wanted ad on the web. Craigslist is a great place to start and it's inexpensive. Thousands of people will see your ad. Be upbeat and positive in your choice of words. "Have fun and earn money caring for pets! Must love animals, be dependable, and provide references." State the hours when you would like applicants to call to schedule an interview.

A word of warning: The folks who answer ads can be an interesting bunch. Weeding out prospects for a job in a pet grooming business can be tricky. Most people have no inkling of how hard the work actually is. You must be totally honest in describing the job to applicants. If they have starry-eyed notions of working with pets, it won't be worth going through the entire hiring and training process, because they won't last long on the job.

Hiring from among your clientele can sometimes be a sticky matter as well. If it doesn't work out, you might lose a customer. Can you really envision that nice poodle-owning lady hefting big dogs in and out of the tub, cleaning up pet hair, and scrubbing that dirty dog who comes in from the farm once a year? Local grooming schools are a good source of employees. The best schools offer placement services for their groomer graduates. Vocational high schools are another possibility. Although the skills taught in their animal sciences program may not train full-fledged groomers, they do teach the basics, and their students are usually willing to work hard in animal-related careers. Online classifieds for employers and prospective employees in grooming are also worth checking out. Visit www.groomers.com (the Pet Groomers Lounge) and www.petgroomer.com.

Another source of employees is your state employment agency. Operated under federal auspices, some 2,500 of these offices exist across the United States. Their services are provided free to both employers and employees and are paid for by payroll taxes. In many offices, computer job banks match jobs with applicants. Vocational and professional schools, high schools, and colleges may also be a good resource. Schools normally have placement counselors, and some maintain job bulletin boards. Again, referral services are free.

Because of the ever growing demand for trained groomers, some shop owners are now helping to underwrite the cost of grooming school for a bather or grooming assistant who demonstrates the potential to become a full groomer. If you consider this route, have your attorney draw up an employment agreement to work out terms of employment once the person finishes school.

The Art of the Interview

When a potential employee shows up, have him or her complete an application form. Review the questionnaire and ask any relevant questions regarding previous employment. If the person looks like a serious prospect, check references thoroughly. Now is the time to set your hiring policy, determining how many references you will require and how much background checking you will do.

During the interviewing process, you will have the opportunity to assess the applicant's appearance and demeanor. Is the person clean and well groomed? Did he or she show up on time? Would you feel comfortable having this person represent your business? Ask questions about previous experience and the applicant's own relationships with animals. This will help break the ice, and you will learn about the person's social skills, personality, and intelligence.

As an employer, you are not legally entitled to ask questions regarding age, racial or ethnic background, religious affiliation (including what church an applicant attends or what religious holidays he or she observes), national origin, native language, marital status, number and/or ages of children, provisions for child care, pregnancy or child-bearing issues, general medical condition or state of health, or any non-job-related physical data.

Another subject in which care is required is in asking applicants if they are handicapped. The definition of *handicapped* under federal law is very broad. For example, people are handicapped if they have a mental or physical condition that substantially affects their ability to perform one or more major "life activities," if they have a record of such a problem, or if the employer thinks they have such a problem. In addition, courts have ruled that obesity, suicidal tendencies, post-traumatic stress syndrome, diabetes, and sensitivity to tobacco smoke are all handicaps protected by federal or state law.

Under federal law, alcoholics and drug addicts are also considered to be handicapped and protected by antidiscrimination laws unless their condition currently prevents them from performing a job adequately. Most states have decided that AIDS is a physical handicap entitled to protection under antidiscrimination laws, just as are other communicable diseases. Asking applicants whether they carry the AIDS virus and screening them out of the work force is illegal in many jurisdictions. Although federal law does not in all cases prohibit asking job applicants if they have a particular handicap, some courts have ruled that such questions may be illegal. State laws vary as to what employers may or may not ask. You will be on safer legal ground if you follow the more stringent of the two laws, be it state or federal. You can learn more about such statutes by contacting your state and federal Department of Labor or checking with the SBA online at www.sba.gov.

In your eagerness to fill the position, don't rush the interviewing process. You need to explain job duties and responsibilities fully, presenting a truthful description of your business and the job. This will help you avoid workers who become disillusioned after a few days, wasting your time and theirs. Don't dwell on the negatives, however. You could end up talking the person out of the job before giving it a chance.

You can use your help-wanted ad as a foundation and expand on it for interviewing purposes, using the criteria you stated that you are seeking as a starting point and moving on to the particulars. Listen to what the applicant has to say, offering plenty of time to talk. This will put the person at ease and help you gather information. Try to avoid phone calls and other interruptions during the interview. Keep an open mind, and look for the applicant's positive attributes and strengths. The best employees are those who are motivated and enjoy what they do. Your task is to find people who want to do the job for which they are hired. Be up-front about salary and benefits and let the person know the next step in the process.

Don't leave applicants hanging. Extend the kind of courtesy you would give to one of your clients. If someone has taken the time to come in and fill out an application, you should take the time to respond. As was the case in the interviewing process, to protect yourself against charges of discrimination, you need to be careful in telling applicants why you did not select them for the job if they request such information. You are on the safest footing when you offer a general response, basing your selection on experience, availability, willingness to work, and a positive attitude, or simply stating that you are continuing the search process.

Make sure you provide the prospective employee with a complete job description so later you won't have to hear "You never said I had to do that!" You should probably steer clear of the delicate soul who will balk at pooper-scooping the potty walk or cleaning up the mess that big dog just made in his crate. You'll need the employee to know his or her responsibilities regarding caring for equipment, safety rules, end-of-the-day cleanup, and the correct way to answer the phone.

Training for Success

Because all pet grooming occupations involve safety issues for both animals and their caretakers alike, intensive training is required for each and every employee. Most entry-level pet grooming workers have no idea how hard we work in this field; having them spend a day or two observing what the job entails is a good idea. Walking new hires through the process of their job requirements is the first step in the training process.

You should institute your own checkpoints during the training process. If you notice bad habits developing, take the first opportunity to nip them in the bud. Be tactful in your corrections, explaining the reason behind your methods. In the grooming shop, the biggest dangers in pet handling involve leaving pets unattended in the tub or on a grooming table, and the chance of pets escaping. No dog or cat should ever be allowed to run free in the grooming shop. A dog that is taken out for a potty run must be leashed and wearing a training collar. Vigilant monitoring of pets under the dryer is also a must.

Shop Policies

As you grow and hire new people, review your mission statement with them. You need to make sure everyone who works in your business knows your philosophy and agrees to carry it out. If your statement speaks about "beautiful grooming performed with kindness and respect," the last thing you want is someone yelling and swearing at a dog in your establishment. That kind of behavior is decidedly not what you're about!

Your mission statement spells out your personal ideals, and you should never lose sight of that vision. As far as the day-to-day operation goes, you also need to institute shop policies to help the place run smoothly. Those need to be spelled out and understood by employees as well.

Your shop policies may look like this:

1. No smoking. Secondhand smoke is harmful to pets as well as people. If you need a cigarette, have one when you take your break outside and clean up butts.
2. Lunch breaks are limited to thirty minutes. A morning and an afternoon break are each fifteen minutes long.
3. Quiet music is allowed on the radio—classical, New Age, smooth jazz. No rock or rap, please!
4. End-of-the-day cleanup duties are to be shared equally by all employees.
5. Employees are required to wear smocks or similar uniforms. No off-color logos on shirts; no tube tops or beachwear. Shoes must be worn at all times.
6. The telephone is for business use only. No personal calls are allowed without the permission of the owner.
7. Wages are based on ability, attitude, and improvement and will be reviewed on a six-month basis.
8. Because we are booked weeks in advance, employees must provide ample notice for days off and vacation schedules.
9. Physical and verbal abuse of the pets in our care is strictly forbidden and is grounds for immediate dismissal. If a dog is aggressive or unruly, ask for help. In this shop, there is never an acceptable reason to hit a dog.
10. The computer is to be used only for work-related duties. No personal e-mailing or Internet surfing is allowed.

It's your business, and you have the final say over how it is run. Your leadership and management skills will be called into play as your business grows and you grow as a person right along with it.

Learning to Be the Boss

In your new role as the employer, it is up to you to train your personnel in proper handling techniques, teaching them when to ask for help and how to read animal body language that warns us of aggression and fear. It is up to you to set policies on all aspects of your business and make sure that employees adhere to them. Becoming complacent about these issues is the biggest threat to the safety of any pet grooming operation. All workers should have a copy of your policy handbook and should be required to familiarize themselves with it as soon as they join your staff.

For many of us, adapting to the role of "the boss" is not easy. It seems a lot more comfortable to relate to our employees as friends. As the owner of the business, however, the sole responsibility of every decision and every business policy rests with you. You do not need to run your company like a dictator, but it is necessary for your employees to recognize your authority. To gain their respect, you need to conduct yourself as a professional. You can start by not dumping your own personal baggage on your employees. Your business can provide a warm and friendly atmosphere without turning it into a group therapy session.

Small home-run businesses usually mimic the family model, but try to avoid getting too personally involved in your employees' lives. This can be a slippery slope. Someone has to be the boss, and in this case, it's you. Everything that goes on in your shop is your responsibility. If mistakes are made, the buck stops with you. It's important to be a warm and caring boss and to keep the lines of communication open. The feedback we get from our employees can be highly beneficial to the way we operate. But steer clear of giving advice on relationships and other personal matters. You are not Dr. Phil, and personal problems are best left at home.

If you get too enmeshed in an employee's problems, you can end up bending over backward to accommodate that person's agenda. Such issues as transportation, child care, and punctuality are the employee's responsibilities. Acting as a surrogate mom can quickly turn you into a doormat. Always listen to your employees' concerns, but let them know you are running a business and you expect them to be professional in carrying out their duties.

Having a trusted employee who can take the reins in your absence can be a great blessing. Illness, family problems, or just the need for a well-deserved vacation requires that you either close down the business or have a second-in-command in place. Sometimes it is difficult for a shop owner to delegate responsibility. We tend to think of ourselves as indispensable. It takes time and patience to train someone else to walk in your shoes. It goes without saying that the person you select needs to be totally trustworthy and have good people skills with clients and other employees. Although the acting manager can make on-the-spot decisions in your absence, all policy decisions are still up to you. With such a key employee in place, you might find that you can actually own a business and have a life!

How to Pay Employees

In the grooming industry, it seems that there are as many ways of paying employees as there are breeds of dogs. Salary, commission, a combination of both; hourly; even a certain amount per dog—we've heard them all. In addition, some groomers are independent contractors, responsible for filing their own state and federal withholding taxes.

Commission rates vary depending on the skill of the groomer and how much income he or she brings into the shop. The most common rates are 40/60, 50/50, and 60/40, the first figure representing the groomer's share, the second the owner's share. Because the owner usually provides all grooming products and equipment (except clippers, scissors, and blades) and sometimes provides a bather as well, this type of pay seems weighted in favor of the commissioned groomer. If bathers were paid on commission, the typical rate would be 20/80, or 30/70 if the employee provides other support services.

The way you pay your employees is totally up to you. We compensate groomers and bather-brushers with an hourly pay rate. We start a little above minimum wage for entry-level workers and gradually increase the rate as they grow in skill, speed, and responsibilities. In multigroomer shops where pay is based on commission, there can sometimes be intense competition among groomers vying to get the higher-priced jobs. If you are paid by the hour, it doesn't matter which dogs you groom. You will be assured a day's pay. The employer handles withholding taxes, and salaried employees usually get additional perks such as paid vacations, fully or partially paid health and dental insurance, and even paid holidays and retirement plans.

Gone are the days when groomers worked as second-class citizens with virtually no benefits. In today's economy, if you want qualified people, you need to be competitive with other employers, including the big chain stores, who offer benefit packages.

State and Federal Withholding Taxes

If you have employees, you are required by law to withhold federal and state income taxes as well as FICA (Social Security) Insurance. Depending on the size of your payroll, these taxes are due weekly, monthly, or quarterly. If you pay monthly, as we do, federal taxes must be paid by the fifteenth of the next month at a bank that is authorized to handle such deposits, while state withholding taxes must meet that same deadline. (The monthly amounts you pay for both state and federal withholding taxes will be deducted from your amount due when you file quarterly returns as required for both these categories.)

If you have employees, you will also need to file quarterly forms and pay taxes for each of the following items. (We have handed our payroll and withholding tax duties over to a payroll service, a move we highly recommend as your staff increases.)

- Social Security and Medicare taxes (Form 941)
- Federal income tax withholding (Form 8109) to be deposited at an authorized bank or by using the Electronic Federal Tax Payment System (EFTPS)
- State income tax withholding
- Federal unemployment (FUTA) tax (Form 940)
- State unemployment compensation tax

Check with your tax professional or accountant to learn how your business will be affected by federally mandatory health insurance for employees and whether you will qualify for tax credits for any contributions you may provide.

Employees versus Independent Contractors

When it comes time to add employees, you should be aware that there is more than one way to reimburse them. You should not even consider paying them "under the table." That method is fraught with potential problems and is not worth the risk to you or your business. Besides, it's illegal, and Uncle Sam does not take it lightly when he does not get his due. Failure to withhold, collect, and pay required taxes results in back tax assessments along with interest and penalties. Even if the person you are tempted to pay this way is a good friend or relative, things can change in your relationship or other people could become aware of your practices, giving them the opportunity to get you in big trouble.

That leaves us with two legitimate ways to pay staff: either as an employee or as an independent contractor. For an employee you must withhold state and federal income taxes as well as Social Security (FICA) and Medicare, for which you match your employee's contribution. A newly hired employee must fill out a W-4 form, telling you and the IRS how many deductions he or she will be claiming. The lower the number, the more taxes will be withheld.

As far as benefits go—vacation, health insurance, sick days, retirement plans— that is up to you, the employer. Customarily, such perks have not been the norm in the pet grooming field, but as we compete for good workers in today's competitive work environment this is changing. You must also keep abreast of all legislative changes in the domain of universal health care or mandatory health insurance as it affects the small business owner, both on the federal and state level. In any case, the level of benefits you can afford should be discussed with your accountant.

The independent contractor is just what the name implies. Think freelancer. This person may work for more than one employer and is not considered a permanent staff member. It is up to the independent contractor to pay his or her own income taxes and Social Security, making it easier on you when it comes to expenses and paperwork. However, the IRS has stringent rules about workers who fit this classification.

Your accountant can help you in determining whether a worker is an employee or an independent contractor. It is extremely important that you know the legal requirements for classifying your workers. If you incorrectly classify an employee as an independent contractor and are challenged on the matter by the IRS, you can be held liable for employment taxes and have penalties levied against you.

For clarification on how to classify your workers, see IRS Publication 15, Circular E, Employer's Tax Guide, which will fully explain your tax responsibilities as an employer. It is available through the IRS website (www.irs.gov) or by calling the agency at (800) 829-1040.

According to IRS rules, certain workers are considered employees by law for purposes of the Federal Insurance Contributions Act (FICA), the Federal Unemployment

Tax Act (FUTA), and for federal income tax withholding from wages. Unfortunately, pet grooming workers fall into a "gray area" when it comes to these classifications—we are out there on the fringe again! A worker's status is determined by applying the common law test, certain facts that fall into three main categories: behavioral control, financial control, and relationship of the parties. The IRS defines these terms in the following way.

Behavioral control: A worker is an employee when the business has the right to direct and control that worker. The business does not have to actually direct or control the way the work is done, as long as the employer has the right to direct and control the work. For example:

- Instructions: If you receive extensive instructions on how work is to be done, this suggests that you may be an employee. Instructions can cover a wide range of topics. For example: how, when, or where to do the work; what tools or equipment to use; what assistants to hire to help with the work; and where to purchase supplies and services. If you receive less extensive instructions about what should be done, but not how it should be done, you may be an independent contractor. For instance, instructions about time and place may be less important than directions on how the work is performed.
- Training: If the business provides you with training about required procedures and methods, this suggests that the business wants the work done in a certain way, and you may be an employee.

Financial control: These facts show whether there is a right to direct or control the business part of the work. For example:

- Significant investment: If you have a significant investment in your work, you may be an independent contractor. While there is no precise dollar test, the investment must have substance. However, a significant investment is not necessary to be an independent contractor.
- Expenses: If you are not reimbursed for some or all business expenses, then you may be an independent contractor, especially if your unreimbursed business expenses are high.
- Opportunity for profit or loss: If you can realize a profit or incur a loss, this suggests that you are in business for yourself and that you may be an independent contractor.

Relationship of the parties: These are facts that illustrate how the business and the worker perceive their relationship. For example:

- Employee benefits: If you receive benefits, this is an indication that you are an employee. If you do not receive benefits, however, you could be either an employee or an independent contractor.
- Written contracts: A written contract may show what both you and the business intend. This may be very significant if it is difficult, if not impossible, to determine status based on other facts.

Confused? Let me simplify a bit. In general, you are classified as an employee if the employer tells you when, where, and how to work; trains you to perform a service; and sets your work hours. If you have an ongoing relationship with the business, your services are important to its success, you are required to be available full time, and either you work on the premises or the business provides tools, materials, and other equipment for you to carry out your job, chances are you are an employee.

As you can see by these complex distinctions, the difference between an independent contractor and an employee is not always clear-cut, nor is it something to be taken lightly by either the person doing the hiring or the one being hired. For the sake of the financial security of your business, do your homework. This is one area in which expert advice from your legal and financial support team is vital. If you make the wrong decision, an IRS audit could conclude that you must come up with back taxes, provide retroactive benefits, and pay stiff financial penalties.

If you do employ someone as an independent contractor, you need to file a Form 1099 instead of the usual W-2 form provided to regular employees. This form is also used to report payments of $600 or more for services performed for your business by people not treated as your employees, such as fees to subcontractors, attorneys, accountants, or directors; and rent payments of $600 or more, other than rents paid to real estate agents.

For employees you must file Form W-2, Wage and Tax Statement, to report payments such as wages, tips, and other compensation; withheld income; and Social Security and Medicare taxes; as well as advance earned income credit payments. By law, W-2 forms must be provided to each employee by January 31 for wages paid the preceding year.

Your accountant will walk you through this maze of tax requirements. I know it can be intimidating, but take heart and look around you—every other business owner has gone through the same thing. Your trek through this tangle of red tape may test your mettle, but you are not alone as you make your way to that little spot on the horizon you have carved out for yourself: your business.

The Importance of Staff Meetings

Holding staff meetings on a regular basis is another good tool for employee motivation. These meetings allow you to interact with your employees on a personal level, away from the demands of the busy workplace. Schedule them as an early morning coffee klatch or an after-hours pizza party, a potluck supper at your home, or a dinner meeting at a restaurant—after all, it is a legitimate business expense! As your staff grows, you may even consider having a guest speaker come in to make a presentation on any number of topics, from animal care to employee benefits to self-protection techniques. In this way you will be offering in-service education as well as camaraderie.

Your staff meeting is the place to address any ongoing problems you have been experiencing and to provide a forum for employee input. It gives you the opportunity to welcome new staff members and bid a fond farewell to those who leave. It offers a great venue for recognizing employee accomplishments and publicly praising a job well done. To keep your meeting running smoothly, print up an agenda beforehand and make sure everybody gets a copy.

Motivated to Succeed: Praising a Job Well Done

Keeping employees motivated is not as difficult as you might think. It's all about positive reinforcement. Employees' behavior is influenced by the results or consequences of their actions. Those consequences can be either positive or negative. When it comes to motivating your employees, positive works best.

The opposite approach, involving harsh criticism and reprimands, may change people's behavior in the short run, but it doesn't motivate them to maintain the desired behavior for any length of time. Moreover, there is a "punishment effect" involved in making a person feel inferior or ashamed. When the punishment mode is used to control behavior, people perform at a level just sufficient to avoid punishment. They are really not motivated to change.

On the other hand, there are many ways to positively reinforce desired behavior. Recognize your employees' contributions by thanking them, either in public or with a handwritten note. Honor them with awards, from simple certificates you make up on your computer to company T-shirts or jackets, movie tickets, or gift certificates from a nice restaurant. Pitch in to offer your help when they seem overwhelmed; show your concern when they have been working hard; put their pictures on the wall or on your website when they have won an award; give a promotion or a bonus—all of these make an employee feel proud and appreciated, acknowledged as a valued member of your team.

Surveys have shown that praise and recognition boost an employee's performance more than any other measure, including a raise. Communication is critical. Let your employees know how the business is doing and how their efforts are helping you to achieve your goals. Involve them in your decision-making process. Solicit their opinions and encourage them to help shape ideas that will improve the business.

Avoid micromanaging. If you have done your job right, once your employees have moved beyond the training period, you shouldn't need to be breathing down their necks. Step back and let them do their jobs. Be sensitive to their individual differences. Some people require more positive strokes from you than others. Be fair and consistent. Whether you know it or not, word gets around like wildfire when someone gets a raise. Make sure that you review everyone according to the same timetable. No one likes to feel taken for granted or overlooked. Your role as the boss is akin to that of a parent. All the members of your business "family" must feel that they are valued and appreciated equally in your eyes.

Correcting Employee Problems

Bringing personal problems to work, job burnout, personality clashes, the poisoning effect of one negative person—all of these can cause poor morale in your growing business. Behaving like an ostrich with your head in the sand will only make things worse. Employees need to know that you will listen to their problems and concerns and do your best to address them. If a worker is bored within the limits of the job, think about broadening his or her duties and responsibilities. If you get a complaint from a client, always listen to the employee's side of the story. The key to motivating and retaining good employees is to be a good manager. You are the boss, and you set the tone.

Health Insurance and Benefits

One of the primary methods of holding on to good employees is an effective benefits program. Unfortunately, the pet grooming field has lagged behind most other occupations as far as benefits go. According to the 2008 Petgroomer.com industry survey, only 26 percent of grooming businesses offered health insurance to their workers. Now that PetSmart and Petco have entered the world of grooming and offering attractive benefits packages to their staffs, the bar will be raised for everyone else. That is one favorable aspect of the arrival of the corporate chains on the pet grooming service scene.

You need to be aware of the health of your employees. If you notice a good worker undergoing a personality change and the quality of his or her job performance is suffering, it's time to take a closer look. Ignoring psychological problems and substance abuse can be a costly mistake because they can have a direct impact on the atmosphere of your workplace and your productivity. When you select a health care provider, choose one that offers personal counseling for mental health along with provisions for physical illnesses and injuries.

Your policy handbook should plainly state that drug and alcohol use on the job is forbidden and that violation of this policy is grounds for disciplinary action, including dismissal. If your insurance package does not offer counseling, you may want to consider an outside Employee Assistance Program (EAP). These programs provide trained counselors who can offer short-term help and referrals to specialists, if needed. The cost is not prohibitive, usually about $3.50 to $5.00 per month per employee.

Today's most successful business owners and managers are creative and sensitive to their employees' needs. They realize there's more to motivating employees than putting money in their pockets. They are leaders who create a climate in which employees willingly and enthusiastically do their best work. As your business grows, you can move beyond just being the boss to becoming a leader who brings out the best in yourself and your staff.

Closing Thoughts

From Kathy

My career in pet grooming has provided me with many rewards, including a lifetime of loving interaction with pets and their owners and the chance to watch our family business grow and continue into another generation. Pet grooming was in its infancy when we began our business in 1970. It has been exciting to watch it come of age with state-of-the-art equipment, computerization, and the realization that even though we were drawn to it because of our love for animals, it is now part of the $48 billion pet industry, a legitimate business that has come of age.

In purchasing this book, you have taken a small step toward becoming a part of the pet grooming business. The need is there for your services, and I hope we have provided you with some useful knowledge as you begin your career. I hope you will not only uphold the standards of those who have gone before you but build and improve upon them as you take pet grooming to the next level. You will work hard, but you will be rewarded with success, joy, and personal growth as you work toward achieving your own dream.

From Missi

From the days when I napped in the crates with the dogs at the original Village Groomer to today, I have always looked forward to going to work. The animals that my family and our employees have cared for over four decades have helped to shape the person I am today. If anybody at The Village Groomer was having a bad day, my dad would tell them to go pick up their favorite dog and spend a little time with him. That is what the unconditional love of dogs and cats does for us. They help us to refocus and remember what is important, like smiling, laughing, and being spontaneous. As we venture into our 41st year of caring for pets and the people they own, I am grateful for the opportunities this industry has offered my family. I am proud of the many ways in which my late father, my mother, and I have given back to this grooming industry that we love so dearly. I hope you come to love it just as much as we do. I dedicate this book to Guido, the Portuguese Water Dog that taught me to love more deeply than I knew how.

Index

About the Authors

Kathy Salzberg is a freelance writer and a National Certified Master Groomer who has been in the pet industry since she joined her late husband, David, at the Village Groomer in Walpole, Massachussetts, in 1976. Since his death in 1996, she has run the grooming salon and retail pet supply store in partnership with her daughter, Missi Salzberg, who is a well-known industry writer and speaker. Kathy is also the mother of David and Peter Salzberg and grandmother of Allison, Cara, Kaitlin, Quinn, and Dylan Salzberg and Ethan Withrow.

Born in Boston, Massachussetts, Kathy has written about grooming and pet grooming issues in such publications as *Cat Fancy, Popular Dogs, Puppies USA, Dogs USA, Kittens USA, Cats USA,* and *Pet Age.* For six years she wrote a humor column for *Groom & Board* magazine, for which she was twice awarded the Cardinal Crystal Achievement Award as Grooming Journalist of the Year. She has also written *The Everything Small Dogs Book,* to be published by Adams Media, and was a contributor to *The Dog Bible,* published by Bowtie Press. She lives with her beloved pets in Walpole and Eastham, Massachusetts.

Missi Salzberg is the current owner of The Village Groomer & Pet Supply and Dog Daze Day Camp. She has been involved in the professional pet grooming industry her entire life, growing up working the groom room and retail shop with her parents. Missi has been nominated for the Cardinal Crystal Achievement Award for journalism three times, winning the award in 2008 and happily losing once to her mother! Missi is an Oster Ambassador and does private consulting. She has presented programs at many of the national grooming trade shows. She emcees her home show for the New England Pet Grooming Professionals each fall. Missi has written for several industry magazines, including *Grooming Business* magazine.